To my wife, Pat, who has been both compass and critic of this work, and the best editor I'll ever have. And to my two sons, John David and Daniel, who inspired me to do this book now, before I become the third best writer in the family.

21 Things
I Wish My
Broker
Had Told Me

Frank Cook

Practical Advice for New
Real Estate Professionals

Dearborn™
Real Estate Education

While a great deal of care has been taken to provide accurate and current information, the ideas, suggestions, general principles, and conclusions presented in this text are subject to local, state, and federal laws and regulations, court cases, and any revisions of same. The reader is urged to consult legal counsel regarding any points of law. This publication should not be used as a substitute for competent legal advice.

Senior Vice President and General Manager: Roy Lipner
Publisher: Evan M. Butterfield
Development Editor: Christopher Oler
Production Manager: Bryan Samolinski
Creative Director: Lucy Jenkins

Published by Dearborn™ Real Estate Education
a division of Dearborn Financial Publishing, Inc.®
155 N. Wacker Drive
Chicago, IL 60606-1719
http://www.dearbornRE.com

Printed in the United States Of America

10 9

Library of Congress–Cataloging In Publication
Cook, Frank.
    Twenty-one things I wish my broker had told me/Frank Cook.
        p. cm.
    Includes index.
    ISBN 0-7931-5437-5
        1. Real estate business–Vocational guidance–United States.
I. Title: 21 things I wish my broker had told me. II. Title.

HD1375 .C624 2002
333.33′023′73–dc21   2002025970

Chapter 6
It's Your Money   43

Invariably, new real estate agents misjudge how much money they need to survive the early days of their careers—and those "early days" can be as long as eight or nine months.

Chapter 7
Market Thyself—First   51

It is a strange business, real estate. It's not at all like any profession you've experienced before.

Chapter 8
Do You Know Where You're Going?   57

I wish I had realized earlier how much control I had over the direction of my career.

Chapter 9
Family Matters   62

So let's be realistic. Do families and a real estate career mix? Can you get to where you want to go professionally without sacrificing your personal life?

Chapter 10
Working with Friends and Family   68

Memorize this chapter, then rip it out of the book. Then burn the pages and scatter the ashes.

Chapter 11
Competitors and Predators and You   74

In California, not that long ago, two agents from the same company—each with a competing buyer—were making bids to buy the same home.

There's good news, bad news, and good news. The good news is that you're either getting or have gotten your real estate license. The bad news is—oh, lets just face it—you're a real estate agent.

If you let it, the real estate business will make you a better person.

Just as an interesting exercise, and you can do this even on your first day on the job, collect as many business cards as you possibly can.

Two of the more interesting relationships you'll develop during your career are the ones between you and the lawyers representing your clients and the one between you and the home inspectors who comb through houses looking for problems.

Unlike in the past, suddenly there seems to be a no "wrong way" to do real estate.

For years, every personal computer delivered with Microsoft Windows has come with a small group of games that includes the ever popular time-waster Solitaire, and a much less noticed game called Free Cell.

Chapter 18

You and the Gurus of Salesmanship 128

As you've probably already heard, it's true that even after you have your license, you're never out of school in the real estate business.

Chapter 19

To Tech, or Not To Tech? 138

Here's a bit of good news. You're in the real estate business at a perfect time—at least a perfect time in terms of technology you need to get the job done in today's world. If you had started yesterday, you would have been way too early. Had you waited until tomorrow, you'd have been way too late. But today is technologically perfect.

Chapter 20

Practice Good Habits 147

In real estate, like most other enterprises, good habits lead to good business—and bad habits lead to poor business, and maybe even no business at all. It's a difficult job under the best of conditions, and it doesn't help if you fall into habits that lead to self-destruction.

Chapter 21

You've Just Been Asked To Commit a Crime. What Do You Do Now? 155

This chapter is short because I'm in a race with your attention span.

Chapter 22

The Future: Lots of Questions, No Answers 160

Here's the downside. Everything is about to change. Yes, everything. Well, not how many rods are there in an acre, but everything else. Gone. Kaput. Not going to be the same anymore.

I f you're reading this book with the hope that it is *the book* that will make you an instant success in real estate, a bit of warning: That book probably doesn't exist. If you're reading this book with the hope of becoming more comfortable with the real estate industry and maybe gaining a few insights and picking up a few tips along the way, you're reading the right book.

In the years I've covered the real estate industry as a reporter—more than 15 years at this writing—I've made a number of observations about the business and have come to a number of conclusions, but none more fundamental than these:

1. There simply are no shortcuts on the road to real estate success. You have to do the work. *But . . .*
2. There are no speed limits on that road, either. You can move as far as you can, as fast as you can, and no one is going to stop you.

The purpose of this book is to get the new sales associate into the passing lane as quickly as possible, whether you're just starting out or even if you're down the road a ways.

Over the years, I've talked to thousands of real estate professionals, from secretaries to sales associates; from brokers, owners, and managers to educators, lawyers, and regulators. I've talked to many people with lofty ideals. And I've talked to a few rogues, too. What I've found is that there are many pathways into the real estate business and not a single one of them is a guaranteed success . . . or a guaranteed failure.

A well-educated, midlevel executive from another profession who comes into real estate seems to have no better shot at making it big than a former housewife who thinks she'd like to make a bit of money now that the children are gone. Students straight out of college seem to do no better—and no worse—than senior citizen retirees. And foreign-born people, who might think seeking a new career is a difficult prospect, can as easily find a home in the American real estate business as anyone else.

At one time, the industry's "Presidents' Clubs" and "Million-Dollar Circles" were populated by middle-aged white men and women. Today, African Americans, Hispanics, Asians, Indians, and others seem equally able to find their futures in this profession.

But they're also equally able to fail.

That is one of the most interesting features of this business. The normal filters just don't seem to figure in. Being at the top of your class doesn't mean much. Nor does being at the bottom, provided you can pass the exam. The nation's top real estate educators agree that there is just no way of knowing by simply looking out into the classroom which students will succeed in the business and which ones will not. Much depends on your personal motivation, how aggressive you are, your personality, and what model of selling you follow.

Even more bothersome, test scores on state exams are not a good indicator. A high test score does not necessarily mean success. Even passing the exam on the first attempt does not mean you will thrive as a sales associate. Many people try and try again to pass the exam and feel like complete failures. Yet once they do pass and receive their license, within a year and a half, some are out there selling millions of dollars' worth of real estate.

Go figure.

Throughout this book you will find insights, stories of opportunities taken and opportunities missed, and even a few stories about what can only be described as lucky breaks; however, while this information will give you a general idea on how others get the job done, I suspect you'll find that the essence of success in real estate has less to do with your ability to "find" opportunities than your ability to "create" them. And, as always seems to be the case, the harder you work the luckier you will get.

Now, before you go any further, remember: *You can do this.*

Acknowledgments

No book gets written by itself, and this one is no exception. In addition to the many individual professionals you'll find quoted here, who contributed their time and insight to helping others have a better chance at success, there are others whose contributions should be noted. Particularly, Pat Remick, a good real estate professional and great mother-in-law, and John Rice, a good real estate professional and a great neighbor, whose collective honesty about the industry has contributed immeasurably to the construction of this work. I'd also like to thank Tom Hathaway, founder of the Buyer's Agent, for a decade of conversations that helped me form the right questions; and the subscribers to my Real Estate Intelligence Report, who have always helped me come up with the right answers.

Chapter 1

In Conclusion...

I wish I knew now what I will know then

I know this is difficult, but as you stand at the threshold of your real estate career, I'd like you to project yourself seven or ten years into the future, and from that vantage point look back at what you will have learned from being in this business. If you've been in the business awhile, think back on who you were at the start and what you expected.

I'd like you imagine yourself a successful veteran: You've done hundreds of deals, your career already is over the early bumps and bruises, and you're steaming ahead quite nicely now. In fact, you are such a success that your supervising broker has asked you to spare a few minutes to come down to the office and make just a few quick remarks to the latest class of new licensees. The title of your remarks: "I wish I had known then what I know now."

If you can imagine yourself in that position, what do you think you'd tell those new licensees? What warning signs would you post? I suspect you would end up offering them a mix of practical and philosophical insights. I suspect you would present them with a list that would go something like this:

1. I wish I had realized that the real estate business found me, I only thought I found it. Who I was and what I was

doing before I got into real estate were completely irrelevant to the success I could become.

2. I wish I had known what to do those first days in the office when everybody else looked so busy and I felt so out of place. I wish I had known how I could work my way into the mainstream quicker.

3. I wish I had known the difference between being an "independent contractor" and being "free to do whatever I wanted." I didn't understand the need for discipline and standards.

4. I wish I had known earlier what kind of business skills I needed—what kind of salesmanship worked and what didn't. I wish I had known how to move aggressively toward my first transaction.

5. I wish I had known how much money I would need to stockpile before I got into the business and how long it would be before I got my first commission check. I wish I had known how much money I would be spending to get my business going.

6. I wish I had known from the very beginning that I needed to market *me* every bit as much as I marketed my company and my listings. I could have secured my career much earlier.

7. I wish I had understood from the beginning that my colleagues could be both good friends and tough competitors, and that no one owns the business—not them, and not me.

8. I wish I had realized sooner that I needed a niche to call my own, and that if I couldn't find one, I could create one if I just looked around a bit.

9. I wish I had been realistic about the kind of strain my spouse and children would be under if I did the things I felt it would take to become successful. I wish I had remembered that I needed to take time out for them.

10. I wish I hadn't been so frustrated when my own friends and family would deal with someone other than me. It was as much my fault as theirs.

11. I wish I had learned the tricks of the trade earlier and had-

n't been so naïve as to believe competitors wouldn't undermine me if they found the opportunity to do it.

12. I wish I had realized sooner that the general public had such a low estimation of me and my profession, but that I could turn that to my advantage.

13. I wish I had figured out sooner that I needed to continue to support my community and that, in ways that were unimaginable, my community would in turn support me.

14. I wish I had paid attention earlier to those initials on other agents' business cards and understood the value of those designations.

15. I wish I had figured out earlier my relationship to the deal killers—the lawyers and home inspectors—and understood they were just trying to do their jobs.

16. I wish I had known that the real estate business was not fixed in concrete and there were many ways to do business and many ways to make money. I wish I had understood earlier that imagination, ingenuity, and hard work were more important elements in my success than family background or even formal education.

17. I wish I had figured out earlier what a good sales coach could mean to my career, my income, my lifestyle, and my life.

18. I wish I had a better perspective on what technology could do for me, as well as what it couldn't do for me.

19. I wish I had realized earlier the importance of developing high-quality work habits and realized that I could destroy my own career far more quickly than my competitors could.

20. I wish I had consistently understood the importance of allowing people to make their own choices in finding a place to live and that my assumptions were completely irrelevant.

21. I wish I had celebrated the fact that everything in real estate is changing and that every day presented both a challenge and an opportunity to stay ahead of the industry.

I know this may seem like an unusual way to start. It's a little like blurting out the punch line before you tell the joke. But these are the ideas we're going to deal with over the next couple of hundred pages and it's important to see them upfront.

Yes, there are 21 of them. But there could as easily have been 30 or 50, or as easily have been 7 or 10. It's hard to know what's going to be relevant in your career, especially since you're just starting it. When you're just starting it, the best thing about a new career is that it is full of possibilities and empty of regrets.

The worst thing about a new career is that nagging feeling that you probably have unrealistic expectations about the business, and even your ability to be a success in it. Don't worry, you're in good company. You are in good company if you succeed because you can make a very nice living from real estate. And if you appear to fail, you're in good company there, too. The industry itself believes that 9 out of every 10 real estate licensees are basically just muddling through. Somewhere between 15 and 25 percent of people with real estate licenses leave the business every year, unable to make enough money to sustain themselves. About 10 percent of the people in the industry are making a nice living.

Can you be among the 10 percent? Of course.

Will it be hard to do?

In this book, we'll find out what people who've gotten there have to say about that.

No matter how long you stay in the business, whether a few days, a few years, or the rest of your life, you are going to meet some very nice people, and a few very strange ones—many of whom will be your colleagues and clients.

Now go to work.

Thought: If you're reading this as you're in school or about to take the license exam, take a moment to write down a few goals, like "List five houses in the next 12 months" or "Earn $35,000 in my first full year." Then set higher goals for your second year in business and your third. Now take the piece of paper and put it in a drawer somewhere and forget about it. If you're already practicing, try to remember what it was you *would* have written on that piece of paper, if you'd written it, now that you've found it in the back of a drawer.

How Did You Get in Here?

(More important, why did you get in here?)

Being a real estate agent is not a typical childhood dream. People dream of being actors and actresses, professional and Olympic athletes, and they might even dream of becoming doctors or lawyers. In the years I've been writing about this business—first as a wire-service reporter, then as a syndicated columnist, and currently as publisher of my own industry newsletter—I've talked to thousands of real estate professionals and probably asked the same basic question a thousand different times: "What drove you to get into the real estate business?"

Usually, I will get back a kind of blank stare or maybe a quizzical look. After a moment, I typically get a response such as, "Well, nothing, really. Nothing 'drove' me into real estate. I just kind of ended up here."

What often happens is that they were looking for a job, looking for something where they could make pretty good money, looking for something that looked like something they could do. And they found real estate.

In short, and with rare exceptions, most people—even the most successful ones—more or less stumble into this business. It's not a childhood dream, not a first choice of career, and something that very few people are "driven" toward when they first enter the business. Getting a real estate license and trying out a new career is more a matter of necessary change than devotion.

Why Am I Here?

Here are some typical responses to the question "What drove you into real estate?"

- "I was looking for a job."
- "I had a friend who was already in the business."
- "My husband got transferred here, and I needed something to do."
- "I just got downsized."
- "I just got a divorce."
- "My youngest finally moved out."
- "I'm going to do this until I can get this other thing going."
- "Oh, I love houses."
- "I love to help people."

And my favorite response to this question: "Oh, this is just a hobby." With the possible exception of some young adults whose parents already were successful in the business, very few people crave real estate as a career choice. So if your answer to the question "Why did you get into real estate?" isn't packed with enthusiasm, it doesn't necessarily mean you won't be a roaring success.

But the surprise is how many people—after just a few years in the business—will tell you they can't imagine doing anything else. They bloom in a business they never were really convinced they'd like. They planned a brief stop and ended up staying forever. The real estate business is not something you grab, it's something that grabs you.

For those who develop a passion for the business, income becomes almost a secondary factor. The overriding reasons people stay in real estate are that they "enjoy the people" or "enjoy solving the problems." Because of this, people who stay in this business for a long time begin to redefine their position in real estate transactions. They stop describing themselves as "real estate agents" and begin to consider themselves as "consultants" or as "problem solvers." They see their role more as that of an advisor than a salesperson.

Consumers tell you where they want to go and you take them there. They really don't want to know what route you took, what kind of gas you put in the car, or what type of engine is under the hood. They just want to get to where they're going and to get there safely. The quicker you begin seeing yourself in that role, the happier and the more successful you are going to be.

Who Wants to Sell Real Estate?

The reality seems to be that nobody is born to sell real estate, but there are some curious indicators about who might be successful. If you look back over the years of modern real estate practice—which you can roughly trace back to somewhere in the 1950s—nobody who taught real estate, nor even anyone who owned a real estate brokerage, could point to a brand new agent and say, without fail, "That person is going to be a success. That person is going to sell a lot of houses."

Some incredibly nice people have come into this business, as well as some incredibly smart people and some incredibly dynamic people. For those who failed, invariably what pushed them out of the business was their inability to carry a deal all the way to its conclusion—their consistent inability to deliver a product (in this case a house) to their client. If you do not have the patience to take a client all the way to the conclusion of the deal—if you can't stay with the deal, nail down the loose ends, handle the problems that come up, and make sure everything is tied together—then you are going to have a difficult time in this business.

High-powered businesspeople, who are used to delegating authority, often do not make good salesmen because they're not used to dealing with the details of the transaction. You simply cannot depend on someone else to do the paperwork. Starting out, at least, you are not going to be the "big picture guy" who puts the deal together with details to be worked out by a helper. *You* are the transaction. In fact, it is because of that need to be the constant shepherd of the deal that has caused some interesting, and perhaps unsuspecting, people to do quite well in this business.

- Moms who have just sent their last child off to college often do well in real estate.
- Flight attendants looking for a bigger paycheck will often find one selling houses.
- Nurses who get burned out in the medical profession are often successful.
- Teachers going into retirement often get the job done.

The common thread seems to be that all these people are trained, conditioned, or in some way required to put someone else ahead of themselves. Whether it's children, passengers, patients, or students, these are people who are on the front line of having to deal with someone else's problems. If they do not resolve the problem quickly and conclusively, odds are the problem will not get solved.

New Developments…

Today's top recruits in the real estate business continue to be that core group of people who are trained to put others before themselves. But new types of people are being added to this core group as well. Middle-level executives downsized by their companies are trying real estate. They like the idea of being the master of their own fate. They enjoy the notion of controlling their own hours, marketing their own ideas, and having their level of income directly related to their level of work. College students joining the business straight out of school represent a new faction of real estate professionals. The reason for this phenomenon is harder to pin down. In the late '90s, the heyday of the economic boom, American industry was recruiting hard for top workers. Signing bonuses were being paid to students the minute they stepped down from the graduation platform. Some students did-n't even bother waiting for graduation, leaving early to start lucrative careers. At the end of the decade, however, the bubble burst. Layoffs began hitting across all economic sectors. Campus recruiting died down. Signing bonuses diminished. The result, some say, is that many college students—looking around from that graduation platform—saw the biggest paychecks going to sales-people in a variety of industries. Real estate suddenly didn't look so bad.

The question, of course, is whether looks can be deceiving.

Three Quick, Unfinished Stories

Here are three quick stories to give you a glimpse of where you can expect to be—and what you can expect to be thinking—within a fairly short period of time. I call them "unfinished" because I really don't know if any of these people will still be in business by the time you read this.

Sarah at Two Weeks

Just two weeks after getting her license and going to work, Sarah loved real estate. No, she hadn't made any money yet, but she was going through her broker's training courses and was "shadowing" a top producer. She did have a lead, however, and she felt there was a good possibility of making her first sale within a couple weeks.

Although she didn't realize it, Sarah was an extraordinary fit for the real estate profile: She was in her late 40s, her children were nearly grown, she was a trailing spouse—her husband had been transferred to the city—and she wanted to find something to do. She had been a teacher earlier in her life, and she spoke some Spanish, though in her particular market that was not a major plus. It was, however, something the company owner thought might prove useful someday.

However, while she fit the profile, I doubted that was the rea-son she started in real estate. So I asked her, "Why real estate?"

"I've had several friends who are real estate agents, and I've listened to them talk about the business. I guess I've always been a little intrigued, not as much with being an agent as with meeting people and getting involved with them under some pretty stressful situations. I'd like to know if I can handle it."

She'd also had the benefit of having been through the real estate process on the consumer side a few times, and didn't much care for the agents she and her husband had hired.

"The first thing we bought was a condo that was being built. We asked the agent for some changes and the agent said, 'No problem.' But when we were ready to close, none of the changes had been made. The builder had said 'no,' and the agent didn't tell us. The agent kept saying we were bound by the contract, and we were stuck with the condo. I don't want to be that kind of agent. I want to help my clients get what they want."

Looking back on her prelicense class, Sarah was disappointed with her fellow students. "The other people in the class weren't very professional," she observed.

Also, she thought her instructor was very poor—until after she passed the exam.

"All he did was teach the law. We tried to ask 'What if' questions, and he wouldn't talk about them. He said his job was to teach us things that would help us pass the test. He said 'What if' questions would just distract us."

She was frustrated at the time, she said, but she passed the test the first time. "What if" questions, she now realized, were best left to on-the-job training.

Her first real assignment came from the top producer she was working with, a research task to match the best school to a client. "We talked about the client, and [the top producer] said we should each come up with a list of schools where we thought the family might be happy." Fortunately, her list and the top producer's list paralleled very closely, and Sarah moved a step closer to being sent off on her own. "You do the legwork and the research in the beginning to make sure the job is done right," she said. "I've been working 10 to 11 hours a day. But [the top producer] is working 11 to 14 hours per day." Still, she said, she was anxious to start doing her own deals and making money.

Thanks to her husband's income, they're "not great, but okay," she said. "It's a little tight. The cost of getting into business was overwhelming to me. I sank $320 in the course. There are fees for everything: a fee for the license, a fee for joining the state REALTORS®, a fee for the MLS, insurance, and they're already talking about the fee for continuing education classes. It's a lot more than I expected."

Sarah is in a good place. True, she's only been at it for two weeks, but already she feels comfortable with the business. She has the right attitude, doesn't mind the long hours, and seems to be working with a good mentor. There's no saying whether Sarah will be a success, but the early indicators say that she will.

Jim at Six Months

At the very least, Jim was worried. He already could tell that in the not-too-distant future—maybe a matter of weeks—he would have to make a decision on whether to pull the plug on his six-month career in real estate. More likely, the decision would make itself. Jim became a real estate agent almost straight out of college. His reasons for getting in were pretty straightforward: Jobs at megacorporations with megasalaries had dried up, replaced by the era of low salaries being offered to new employees, all of whom had to start at the bottom.

A real estate career in a lucrative market could mean more money, and that money could come in faster than anything available anywhere else. At least that's what he thought.

Now he isn't so sure.

He was still waiting for his "first" deal to close. Oh yes, he had closed his second, third, and fourth deals, but the very first deal he ever worked on "has turned into a real pain in the butt." He represented the buyers, and the buyers' lawyer was "nit-picking the deal to death."

"He won't let it close," Jim said. "Every time we set a date, he comes up with a problem at the last minute. The sellers are angry, the listing agent is angry. The buyers aren't saying anything other than, 'We trust our lawyer.' This thing is going to kill me."

At best, Jim had mixed feelings about his career choice. "I've met a lot of dishonest people—not break-the-law dishonest, but more like don't-trust-them dishonest. You think you are working together [with an agent from another company] and getting things done, and you are doing your end. But then you find out they didn't hold up their end. It's like they are milking you for your work."

Jim's frustration was evidenced by his oft-repeated statement, "You don't get paid unless it closes." Throughout the interview, he would work the phrase into the conversation. "You may have four or five clients out looking for homes, making offers and receiving counteroffers, but you can't count your chickens before they hatch. You don't get paid unless it closes."

Jim's frustrations don't begin and end with buyers and lawyers. Talking generally about buyers, sellers, and other agents, he just shook his head. "A lot of people don't care if they're wasting your time. I think it's even worse because I'm new to the business."

Jim has closed some deals, and he has a base of understanding about the real estate business; however, he doesn't seem happy. To make it in this business, you have to like it—even love it. He's given it a whirl for six months, and he has found it's not what he expects. This could happen to anyone, no matter if they do everything right or everything wrong for those first six months.

Sam at Ten Months

Sam had received his license about ten months earlier, and the two biggest questions I had for him were, were: "Do you like the business so far? Are you making any money?"

He answered yes to the first question—he still liked the business. As for the question about money, he responded sadly that no, the money wasn't coming in very quickly.

He was 25 and already had moved from one real estate job to another—not necessarily a bad sign but not a very positive one, either. He had started off as a salesman for a builder. He already had stopped doing that and had gone to work for a broker. He was now working in a nice-sized brokerage office in an urban setting. He was still fairly confident.

"I just want to make enough money to have a comfortable living," he said. "This is a great market. It's hard work but it's doable." Like many other new licensees, he suggested, "This is just a temporary job. There's something else I really want to do."

Working for a builder had its advantages. It was a more structured atmosphere with a defined list of properties to sell. Moving to a brokerage office was an entirely different set of challenges. "You need a lot more dedication. You need to be able to work on your own. I also found I had to learn, and relearn, a lot of things I didn't need to know at the builder. I didn't have to do a lot of the paperwork. Now I do."

Like many beginning agents, Sam was trying to build his business by contacting people who already were trying to sell their homes themselves (For Sale by Owner—sometimes called *FSBOs*). He was attempting to convince those FSBOs that they would be better off—get a better sale, quicker, and for more money—using a real estate professional than trying to go it alone.

He was being only marginally successful.

Most of the FSBOs on his list already had been contacted many times over by other real estate agents hoping to list the house. FSBOs often told him that they would be happy to pay him some money if he brought them a buyer. They were only trying to avoid the listing portion of the commission.

Sam also was working from his sphere-of-influence list—a list of members of his extended family and a number of his friends. When he entered the business, he had about four months' worth of living expenses tucked away. He was going through it fast, but believed he was closing in on his first transaction for the brokerage. Essentially, he will have been in the real estate brokerage sales business about six months before he gets his first paycheck.

Sam has worked hard, but sometimes working smart is better. Luckily, he had some money set aside to get through the early bumps and bruises of the business (a good idea for all new salespeople). While Sam might not be experiencing early success, he has accumulated some good experiences, and though he has made some mistakes, he seems to be ready to change his luck.

Thought: It's never too late, or too early, to go back to the basics. A little later you'll read about a top producer who is now one of the best selling agents in the Coldwell Banker system. Even now, he constantly works the contact list he started when he entered the business.

Chapter 3

Great Expectations

What you can expect your first day at work

I t's 9 A.M., Monday morning. You have a brand-new real estate license in your pocket, and you're standing at the front door of a real estate company—your new employer. What do you do now? Well, let's back up a second. You may have already made your first mistake.

Needless to say, if your supervisor tells you to be there on Monday morning, be there on Monday morning. But in many real estate offices, Monday is exactly the *wrong* day to start work.

Unlike the rest of the world, Monday is not the first day of the week in real estate—it's actually the last day of last week. While the rest of the world uses Monday to ramp up after a restful weekend, real estate uses Monday to wrap up all the work that was done on Saturday and Sunday.

Weekends are big "showing" days, when buyers are out walking through houses and deciding what they want. Buyer agents who wrote offers during the weekend expect to hear back from sellers and their agents Monday or Tuesday. In many cases, deals that were struck during the weekend now have to be wrapped up: There are home inspections to order, financing to be arranged, appraisals to be done, title searches to be set up, and closings to schedule. Monday is when the paper flow of a real estate transaction really begins.

For working agents, Monday is the day to nail down the loose ends. Buyers not quite ready to make offers may have one or two more questions. Monday is the day to get those answers. Also, agents who were sitting on open houses during the weekend use Monday to input contact information collected from people who wandered through. Listing agents who have yet to contact their sellers with feedback from the weekend's showings will be doing that on Monday. All in all, Monday can be a very busy time in a real estate office, and it's not necessarily the best day to start work.

Having said that, however, most of the company's agents are likely to be in the office on Monday, giving you a good chance to meet people. Alternatively, most of the managers are going to be busy going over contracts, working out problems, and talking to the sales staff. If there is a message you should get from all this, here it is: Real estate is not a Monday-through-Friday business. And while Monday might not be the best day to start, plan to come into the office when your supervising broker asks you to. There is much to learn, whether it's Sunday, Monday, or Thursday. Just expect the lessons of each day to be a little bit different.

What You Can Expect in the First 30 Minutes: 9:00 to 9:30

Let's assume your new employer, realizing Monday is not the best day of the week to start training, has you come in on a Tuesday. OK, so it's 9 A.M., *Tuesday* morning. You have a brand-new real estate license in your pocket, and you're standing at the front door of a real estate company—your new employer.

At this very moment, you have no idea how to sell real estate. Teaching you sales skills was not the job of your prelicense instructor. His or her job was to lay down the legal ground rules under which you will operate. Learning sales skills is up to you.

So, what do you do now? Answer: Ask lots of questions—and listen. If you're lucky, the office you've joined has a planned routine that introduces new agents to the business. In your first 30 minutes, that routine probably will include a quick tour of the office, brief introductions to any managers who are in the building, short outlines of what they do, and a number of other things you need to know to get going. Large real estate companies that bring in new agents every month usually have some kind of formal orientation program. Small companies, however, that add only one or two agents per year, probably do not find it worthwhile to maintain a formal training routine. If the office you've joined does not have an introductory program, then you need to bootstrap your own training.

Agent, Train Thyself

As soon as possible, you want to meet as many managers as you can and learn their role in the real estate routine. You need to find your desk and meet the people sitting around you. Needless to say, smile and be friendly. These are the people who are going to help you settle into the business.

Take the opportunity to get the layout of the office. Where are the bathrooms? Where is the coffee machine? Where do you park your car? Where do you get forms? Is there a preferred vendor for business cards, letterhead, envelopes? (This also is a good time to ask someone how the phone system works.) And make a phone call—any call. Call your mom, your spouse—you decide. Announce to whoever is on the other end that you are in your new office. Tell them, "If you know of anyone who wants to buy a house, have them call me at this number."

Congratulations! You've just made your first real estate contact, and you've been at work less than an hour.

Be sure to ask the broker how he or she wants the phone answered. This may sound like strange advice, but do not underestimate the value of understanding the phone system. Within a few days—and maybe a few hours—you may be answering the phone and routing calls all over the building. These are going to be "money" calls that your colleagues are going to want to get. The quickest way to a bad first impression is to transfer a colleague's hot new prospect into oblivion.

Right about now you're probably thinking that all of the above is pretty common sense stuff. You may be wondering why it's included here at all. Here's why. Throughout the history of real estate, new agents have been notoriously untrained—untrained in office policies and procedures, and untrained in the actual art of selling real estate. They literally have been left to fight their way into the industry. Their sales training amounted to, "Here's your desk, here's your phone, congratulations, you're on your own."

It's been only in the past several years that real estate companies have realized the need to do more than show a new agent to his or her desk. If you somehow find yourself in an office that does minimal training, you have to train yourself. If you sit back and wait for training, you're sitting back and waiting to fail. Take the initiative.

From 9:30 until Noon

Start getting into real estate–specific tasks.

Ask if you'll have a mentor you can work with, someone who has been in the office awhile and understands procedures. Ask if you can shadow—literally walk around with—a top producer as he or she goes about their business routine.

Find out about the office computer system. Work with the software awhile and learn what it does and why you need it. Ask your mentor, your supervisor, or even the person at the next desk what happens when you get your first listing. Ask what legal things you need to say to an individual selling his or her house, and what correct answers you need to hear from them before you continue. Find the right form to fill out, and find out whom to give it to. Find out how your listing makes its way to the multiple-listing-service, and find out how it gets from the MLS to the Internet. Find out what Web sites the company puts its listings on and how they get there.

At some point (at least hopefully at some point) someone is going to suggest that you need to read through the office "Policies and Procedures Manual." Find out if you can take it home that night if you promise to bring it back the next day. (If your company has a written policies and procedures manual, which it should, it's something you should read as soon as possible, but read through it when you have time to concentrate on it, not when you're busy with other things and might have a tendency to skim.)

Get copies of company promotional materials, the things the company wants you to hand out on listing presentations or to potential buyer clients. Those materials are going to contain the selling points of the company and its services. Embrace those selling points as your very own, and when you finally do go out on a listing presentation, don't say, "Here's what the company offers," say, "Here are the services we offer."

Training, Training, Training

Sometime early on, if you haven't been told already, ask someone if your company offers any kind of formalized training sessions on how you can learn to be a real estate agent. If the answer is "yes," and there happens to be one starting down the hall in 10 minutes (or this afternoon or tomorrow morning), ask if you could join it. Make up your mind from the beginning that you are going to take advantage of as many training sessions as you can, as fast as you can—especially if they are free.

Find out if the local Board of REALTORS® will be offering any seminars soon. Many times, banks and title companies will offer training on how their products tie into your business. Again, attend as many of those sessions as you can, even if no one else in your office is going.

Why? First of all, you're bound to learn something about your business that you don't already know. Second, it's important for you to hear the language of real estate—the lingo, the sales jargon, and the slang that people in business invariably fall into. Also, it gives you an opportunity to meet other people in the real estate community, to hand people your business card, and to get one from them. You don't have to tell them you are new in the business, but don't hide it if they ask. Simply say you just affiliated with XYZ Realty and leave it at that. Sooner or later, you will realize the importance of networking to your real estate career. You might as well realize it sooner. In the course of your career, you will likely work with agents from other companies as much as you work with agents from your own company. Start building friendships from the beginning. The day is going to come when your marginal homebuyers are going to run up against some stubborn homesellers. Your personal relationship with the listing agent could make the difference between whether or not your client gets the house.

The Rest of the Afternoon

At some point on your first day, a supervisor or colleague is going to suggest that you need to start writing out your sphere of influence list. Your *sphere of influence* literally is everybody you know. Everybody. No, not just everybody you know who might need a house soon. Your sphere of influence is *everybody* you know.

You need to write down your mom's name, along with her mailing address, e-mail address, and phone number. You need to do the same with your dad, your brother, your sister, your aunts and uncles, your friends from grade school, that girl (or guy) you dated in high school, the guy who gave you your first summer job, the parents in your children's play group, and (if you still remember the name) the leader of your Girl Scout or Cub/Boy Scout troop. Everybody. Start with last year's Christmas card list and go from there.

You want to type these names into a computer, preferably into a database program, because you are going to be coming back to them for the next several weeks, months, or even years. These are the people who are going to help you get started in real estate. These are the first people who are going to get a postcard from you announcing that you've joined XYZ Realty.

Sure, you will tell them you'd be happy to sell their house or find them a new house if they're in the market. You certainly don't want to turn down business. But the real reason for contacting the people in your sphere of influence is that you are looking to them to help you find your first clients. Ideally, you contact them. They, in turn, mention your name to the people they know. If you have 50 people on your list, and each one contacts three other people, suddenly you have 200 people talking about you. That's a start.

Some of the people to whom you already sent a postcard you are going to call—not to sell them a house, but just to emphasize again that you have a license and you would appreciate it if they would send their friends to you. However, you might not want to call everyone on the list. There's a fine line between trying to find business and losing business by being a nuisance. Call those who are closest to you or those you have lost touch with and would like to become reacquainted with. Call those people you've been meaning to call, and chat with them about their life as well as yours. Remember, this business is about networking and enlarging your sphere of influence. If you can do this with the help of others, then do it.

As you go through your career, you will find yourself going back to your sphere-of-influence list time after time. You will revise it constantly, adding names, deleting names, putting in past clients and future prospects. Ultimately, you will see it grow to hundreds of contacts—each one of whom could be a business contact. It's important to know this from the start. Get your list started, keep it organized, and most of all, don't be shy about periodically returning to it.

The Next Few Days

For the next few days, you are going to focus on three things: (1) contacting the people in your database; (2) picking up whatever insights, tips, and training are available; and (3) studying the product you're selling—homes.

Grab the real estate section from last week's paper and read through some of the listings. Look at how they are written—how they attract consumers. Spend some time on the Internet searching for homes the way you feel consumers would. In your browser, search for homes in your community using keywords like "homes Kansas City" or "real estate Nashville." See what comes up. Take a look at prices and neighborhoods.

Almost every community has a day set aside for "brokers' open houses," when agents invite other agents to look through homes that they've listed. The purpose of the broker's open house is for agents to go through houses and give the listing agents feedback on the properties they're representing. Here is some common feedback agents give to brokers:

- "There's not enough light in the dining room."
- "The backyard is great!"
- "The children need to clear the clutter from their shelves."
- "The carpet needs to be cleaned or replaced."
- "The kitchen is the main selling point of this house."

The listing agents will take these comments back to the sellers, who can then make changes based on the suggestions, giving them a better chance of selling their houses. This also gives touring agents a first look at homes just coming on the market, so they can figure out if they can match them to their buyers. Overall, the idea is to improve the marketability of the home. As a new agent, you should avail yourself of every opportunity to be around other agents from other companies, handing out business cards wherever you go and getting them in return.

FSBOs and Expireds

In your first few days on the job, your broker may suggest that you go through the newspaper and start contacting FSBOs. Your broker may hand you a list of "expireds" and suggest you start calling them. Expireds are people who have listed a home with another agent, usually at another company, but for some reason the home did not sell during the time of the listing contract.

When the contract expires, you are free to contact the sellers to see if they would like to list a home with you instead. If your boss asks you to do these things, obviously you should; however, make sure you understand that there are positives and negatives to working with both expireds and FSBOs. The positive side is that at least you know these people are in the market to sell their homes. The negatives are that both probably are having bad experiences with real estate agents. Most people decide to try to sell a house themselves either because (1) they don't want to pay a full commission to a real estate agent or (2) they don't like real estate agents. Statistically, the vast majority of FSBO attempts fail and they end up listing with an agent. But they're usually not happy about it. So when contacting the FSBO people, understand their mindset, where they're coming from, and use this knowledge to try to woo them to list with you.

In attempting to recruit expireds, be sure to look at possible reasons the house didn't sell with the first real estate agent. Was it overpriced? (Usually.) Was it poorly maintained? (Often.) Did the first agent really do nothing to market the property? (Occasionally.) Nevertheless, both FSBOs and expireds are worth contacting. I have talked to agents who have made a lot of money by working those lists, and they might work for you, too.

Baby, It's Cold Outside

Contacting FSBOs and expireds is typically known as "warm calling" because you know the person on the other end of the phone has at least some interest in the real estate process. The other end of that kind of marketing is "cold calling." Cold calling is taking a list provided by the broker—or even the phone book— and making call after call after call until you randomly find someone who is interested in buying or selling a house. I have never met an agent who enjoyed cold calling. In all honesty, I have never met an agent who made a lot of money at it. I have talked to many agents who say they wasted months of their early careers doing cold calls with nothing to show for it.

By and large, cold calling is something you need to have the right personality to do—a personality that does not mind being rejected in angry and bitter tones. If your boss doesn't require that you do this, I recommend you use your time in more effective and productive ways.

The First Few Weeks

In most offices, there is something called *floor duty, floor time, up time,* or *opportunity time.* Essentially, this is a block of time when you are the "agent on duty." Customers calling the office who are not otherwise committed to another agent will be transferred to you.

Often those customers will just have questions: How is the market? What are homes selling for in my neighborhood? How big a down payment do I need to put down? Occasionally, however, they will be ready to sell a house, or they'll need someone to help them find a home they can buy. You should take this opportunity to try to turn those people into your clients.

It's important to be friendly and courteous, and make sure the caller hears your name. It also is important for you to try to get the caller's name, phone number, and (preferably) an address. Be helpful and courteous, but explain to them that you'll call them back later with specific answers to their questions. Also, tell them that you'd like to send them some information, and don't forget to include your business card if you send them information. Don't, however, be surprised if the name turns out to be fake and the phone number phony. Many people like to remain anonymous until they figure out what they really want to do. Yes, they will lie to you.

If your supervising broker doesn't bring it up, sometime in the first week on the job ask him or her about opportunities to be the agent on call. Many brokers prefer to have more experienced agents work floor time, so you may not draw an opportunity for a few weeks. But most brokers also try to spread the time around among any agents who are interested. So, if you express an interest, you'll probably get a chance.

Besides volunteering for floor time, consider asking another agent in the office—a busy, successful one—if you can hold an open house for one of that agent's listings. Before you make that offer, however, discuss with your supervising broker whom you should ask. Sitting on an open house for another agent's listings can create a win-win situation. First, experienced and busy agents usually consider sitting on open houses to be a waste of their time. People who come to open houses rarely buy the house they are touring, and they are often not serious buyers at all. For some reason, however, sellers put a lot of faith in open houses and constantly are putting pressure on their agents to hold them. So if you volunteer to hold an open house for an experienced broker, you both win. The experienced broker gets credit from his seller and the day off, and you get another chance to hand out your business card and get the names and addresses of everyone who comes through the house.

So What Do You Do with All Those Names?

On Monday morning, you'll be typing them into your database and giving them a call, saying, "I just wanted to check back and see if you found any houses you liked during the weekend? You know, a house similar to the one you looked at just came on the market in another neighborhood. I'd love to show it to you ... "

However, it's important to talk with the supervising broker before deciding which top producer to volunteer to help. The hard truth is that some agents are more honorable than others. Some experienced agents will, in fact, stick a new agent with a dog of a listing, a place where the owners have been complaining about the lack of showings and a place that's been on the market for a year, and is overpriced and undercleaned. To mollify the owners, the experienced agent will "magnanimously" allow the new agent to hold an open house that almost certainly will draw little traffic and no serious buyers. Hopefully, the supervising broker will steer you to work on an open house where you have at least a chance of making some contacts.

One More Thing

Did you notice that most of your weekend just vanished? Welcome to the real estate business.

Assignment

Get this information in the first 30 minutes of your first day:

- Where is your desk? Who are the people working around you? (Introduce yourself.)
- Where is the bathroom, the coffee machine, and where should you park your car?
- How does the office phone system work?
- Will someone help you learn the computer system?
- Where is the photocopier and is there a charge to use it?
- Where are the office forms kept, and is there someone who will show you how to fill them out?
- Who is responsible for keeping you abreast of new forms?
- Does the company have a training program to teach you to be a salesperson? Will you start the training today?
- What office meetings are you going to be *required* to attend? What meetings will you be *expected* to attend? What meetings are going to be optional?
- Who is your supervising broker? Will you be working with a mentor?
- What fees are you going to be expected to pay? Multiple-listing-system fees? REALTOR® membership fees? When do you have to pay them?
- Is there a recommended vendor for your business cards and other stationery? Are there any blank business cards in the office that you can use until your printed cards arrive?
- Smile. Your new colleagues are actually glad you're there.

Chapter 4

Honk if You're an Independent Contractor

Honk twice if you know what that means

At some point, right or wrong—or perhaps both right and wrong—the real estate profession came to be viewed as a leisure industry. Here was a place where you could go to "work" but still have time to play golf in the middle of the day, pick up the kids at 3 in the afternoon, come in late, and leave early.

You are your own boss, the literature said. You are—magic words coming up here—an "independent contractor." For decades, the industry has been trying to both live up to and live down that reputation.

It's true, you're an independent contractor (IC); however, that does not mean you're free to do whatever you please. This is especially true in real estate, more so than in other IC professions because real estate ICs are guided by a different set of laws than are ICs in other professions. The following examples should help illustrate the unique and demanding nature of real estate ICs.

Note: We're talking here about legal issues: contract law, employment law, tax law, labor relations—legal stuff governed by a complex system of state and federal laws and regulations. Everything said in this chapter is a generalization: You should check with your broker or a lawyer to find out what your particular status is. That said, let's proceed.

Part I: So, I Am an Independent Contractor!

Well, not exactly. In most practical ways, new licensees—and even more experienced licensees—are employees of their companies. Let me restate that: Think of yourself as an employee, but there are some major caveats coming up. In real estate, just as in any other career, your employer can and will make demands on your work. Your supervisor can assign you "floor duty" in the office, where you will handle general calls that come in during the day. You can be assigned to attend sales meetings and host open houses. You may be assigned to sit and make cold calls or even to attend business education sessions.

Your supervisor can and will demand that all your paperwork be in on time and done correctly and in the manner the bookkeeper prefers that it be done. You may be obligated to get a certain number of listings over a certain period of time. You may be obligated to close a certain number of transactions. Performance standards most likely will be set, and if you fail to meet these standards, you can be fired—just as you can from any other job.

The First Step Is the Bottom Rung

As in most other jobs, rookies tend to get the worst chores in the office, such as weekend duty, and then are expected to climb the ladder from there. However, things tend to get foggy the more experienced you become and, far more important, the more successful you are. As you start creating more income for yourself and your company, you will quickly start becoming your own boss. Think of it as real estate's Golden Rule: "He who makes the gold also makes the rule." If someday you reach the top rung of the ladder, will you still have to sit down from time to time with the broker/owner/manager and review your goals and objectives? Probably. But that's in the best interests of both you and your manager. It's always a good idea to make sure your stars and the company's stars line up the same way.

If you become successful in real estate, soon enough you will be your own boss, and you will get to play golf in the middle of the day. But here's why: If there are people at the country club that you hope to do business with, either now or later, your company will want you to be at the golf course. If that's where your deals come from, that's where you should be. And, yes, it's OK to enjoy yourself while you're there.

Likewise, if there is an organization meeting or a luncheon you feel you should attend, odds are good your broker will work with you to make sure you can be there. But do understand what's happening: Your broker wants you to be wherever you feel you can be productive. There is flexibility in this field, but most often it's because it meets both your and your broker's interests—that of making profits.

Your broker expects—and in time you will come to understand—that you are a real estate professional 24 hours a day, wherever you are and whomever you are with. You never know where your next deal will come from. You are always on duty.

So from a work standpoint, remember there is a difference between being "independent" and being "free." You are independent, but you are not free from guidance or performance.

So I'm Not Really an Independent Contractor?

You certainly are, and there is no one in the United States government, specifically the Internal Revenue Service, who will tell you differently. Likewise, there are few people in the executive ranks of the real estate profession who would have it any other way. In this context, *independent contractor* is a legal term that belongs to the IRS.* It defines people who do work for companies but who are not employees.

What's the difference?

Employees get benefits. In most real estate companies, you don't. The IRS has very specific rules about who is an *independent contractor* and who is an *employee*. Elsewhere (but not in real estate), independent contractors are task-oriented. They are expected to achieve a goal, but their manner and methods are not supervised. If the company did control the manner and methods, if an employer directly supervised the contractor on a day-to-day basis, conceivably the IRS could declare that contractor had become an employee.

Why is that a concern? Because if the contractor becomes an employee, suddenly the company is liable for payroll deductions and benefits, workers' comp must be paid, health insurance must be made available, vacation time can be accrued, and things such as severance pay become a concern.

There is none of that for an independent contractor, as defined by the IRS. But now you're thinking, "Then that's not me. My broker has direct supervision over me. He trains me. He can require certain performance standards. Why am I considered an independent contractor?" In a word, "Clout."

Real estate brokers gathered themselves together many years ago and lobbied Congress to declare real estate agents independent

---

*Chapter 23, Internal Revenue Code of 1954, Sec. 31.3306(i)-1: Who are employees?

"In general, if an individual is subject to the control or direction of another merely as to the result to be accomplished by the work and not as to the means and methods for accomplishing the result, he is an independent contractor. An individual performing services as an independent contractor is not as to such services an employee. Individuals such as physicians, lawyers, dentists, veterinarians, construction contractors, public stenographers, and auctioneers, engaged in the pursuit of an independent trade, business, or profession, in which they offer their services to the public, are independent contractors and not employees." IRS Publication 15-A specifically calls real estate agents "statutory non-employees."

An employee is treated as self-employed for all Federal tax purposes, including income and employment taxes, if

1. substantially all payments for their services as direct sellers or real estate agents are directly related to sales or other output, rather than to the number of hours worked, and
2. their services are performed under a written contract providing that they will not be treated as employees for Federal tax purposes.

The term *licensed real estate agents* includes individuals engaged in appraisal activities for real estate sales if they earn income based on sales or other output.

contractors. There was nothing altruistic about it. Broker/owners did not want to have to deal with the paperwork of payroll taxes, nor did they want to provide benefits. They successfully argued that real estate agents really are on their own in terms of how much they can make. Their income (your income) truly was not under the control of the broker. Voila! Independent contractor.

So I Am an Independent Contractor? (Unfortunately, Yes.)

Indeed, you are an independent contractor. And for almost all new agents, that's not necessarily a good thing. Most real estate agents come into this business from other lines of work. They have been schoolteachers or police officers, airline attendants, salespeople in other professions, or maybe midlevel managers. What all those fields have in common is that their employers must make payroll deductions and provide W-2 forms at the end of the year. In real estate, there are no W-2s. Nobody is going to deduct a dime for taxes from your commission check. They probably are not going to contribute to your health insurance. Very rarely do companies offer any kind of retirement benefit. There are no 401(k)s. If you stay in this business, you will become quite familiar with the term *quarterly estimates*.

You are going to have to learn to look below the top line that says you earned $90,000 in commissions last year. The bottom line is going to reflect that 28 percent of that belongs to the government in income tax that hasn't been withheld, and there probably will be a self-employment tax on top of that. A few days before you go into real estate, you'd be smart to talk to an accountant.

Certainly, in some companies, these attitudes are changing. Retirement benefits are becoming an option, and medical insurance is becoming available. Should you become a member of the National Association of REALTORS® or some other professional association, those groups also offer some retirement and insurance plans that can help you out. But by and large, even today, the real estate agent/independent contractors are on their own in terms of financial planning.

Welcome to the New Age

Finally, it needs to be said that the modern era of real estate is beginning to play out as a strange scenario in the independent contractor/broker supervision arena. You need to be aware of what's going on.

An increasing number of brokers are using independent contractor status as a shield against legal liability. Outside the real estate industry, when something gets screwed up and somebody is mad enough to sue, the first person they sue is the guy who sold them the faulty "whatever." Then, they sue the employee's boss and the company behind the boss. This search for the deepest pockets is called *uphill liability*.

In real estate, the notion that liability flows uphill is not necessarily true. On occasion, a real estate agent might screw up a deal and end up being sued by a buyer or seller. The buyer or seller will, of course, try to also sue the agent's boss—the broker—and rope in the company, which in actuality is the only one with pockets deep enough to pay off a judgment.

Recently, however, some brokers have successfully argued that neither they nor their companies have liability for the acts of the real estate agent because, after all, the agent is an "independent contractor." In this day and age, the brokers say, communication with sales agents often is by phone message, fax, or e-mail. Direct supervision, according to them, is a thing of the past. The broker can't be held liable because the broker wasn't even aware of what was going on!

The surprise is that some courts are accepting that argument. The reality is that almost every state in the nation requires that supervising brokers be looking over the shoulders of their sales associates. Real estate commissions nationwide require that brokers look at every transaction that flows through the office and make sure every *i* is dotted and every *t* is crossed.

However, brokers say that they don't see the deals and don't have time to supervise deals. The laws in most states, however, care little about a broker's schedule: If the supervising broker doesn't have time, he or she must make time. Just because the agent is an "independent contractor" for tax purposes does not remove the supervising broker from general liability.

Chapter 5

A Fast Track to Your First Transaction

How to make money in real estate without a mask and a gun

Two quick stories.

1. A woman in Montana gets her real estate license. A week later, everybody else in the office goes to lunch. She has to stay behind to answer the phone. A call comes in. The guy asks if there is any ranch land for sale. She says she's not sure, she'll call him right back. She gathers some listings, calls the guy back, and mails the stuff. A week later, the phone rings. He's flying in on his plane the next morning. He wants her to show him a couple of ranches. Three weeks later, her broker hands her a check for $48,000—her first commission in the real estate business.

2. A woman out west has her license for two days. She's home in the afternoon and walks out to the street to check the mail. A guy is driving by in a brand-new Jeep. He stops. "Excuse me, ma'am, do you know if there are any properties for sale around here?" A few weeks later, she stuffs a $25,000 commission check in her pocket.

The point of these stories? Lightning does strike in the real estate business. And the strange thing is that it happens more often than you'd think. Deals—big deals—will occasionally fall right out of the sky. You can have the worst year of your business life turn around in a heartbeat because the right buyer suddenly walks through the door.

But can you count on it happening to you? Can you count on it happening often enough to earn a living? Can you count on it for your first transaction?

Unfortunately, the answers are no, no, and no.

The Only Way to Get Started Is to Get Started

Whether you talk to sales associates who are brand new or to veterans who have been in the business for years, they will tell you there are few things more important than their first deal. In fact, some sales managers say that if anything, new sales associates press too hard for that first transaction. They become obsessed with it—like when you were nine years old and trying to get your first hit in Little League. You think everyone is looking at you, talking about your lack of success, wondering when you'll fail.

The truth is, of course, nobody is talking about you. Most people are too worried about their own work to worry about how you're doing. The reality is that a lot of really good agents have waited a very long time to close their first transaction. A lot of them even feared they'd have to leave the business before they'd really gotten started. But it doesn't have to be that way. In fact, in the modern real estate office, sales managers are doing everything they can to get their newest agents trained and selling within four to six weeks—not just trained in the philosophy of selling, but actually to have a transaction posted on the company bulletin board and a commission check in the pipeline.

David Etzenhouser ■

Find Out What Works

The first thing you need to know is what works. David Etzenhouser, a residential sales manager for the J. C. Nichols

Residential real estate company in Kansas City, surveyed some of his newer, more successful sales associates to figure out what they did to ignite their careers. To even be asked to fill out one of his surveys, new agents had to have at least $2 million in sales volume, or 20 sales in the first 12 months they were in business. His results—while not scientific—are nevertheless interesting. Following are some of the questions Etzenhouser posed to new agents after their first year in business, along with their responses.

Questions	Answers
What was the approximate number or days you worked per week?	On average, 6.27 days per week
What was the approximate number of hours you spent in the office per day?	4.29 hours in the office per day
What was the approximate number of overall hours worked per day?	7.85 hours worked per day
How long did it take for you to feel comfortable in the business?	Approximately eight months
What was your main source for buyers?	(from best source to worst): 1. Personal acquaintances 2. Floor duty 3. Open houses 4. Social group 5. Networking 6. Cold calling 7. Model homes 8. Expireds
What was your main source for sellers?	(from best source to worst): 1. Friends and relatives 2. Social farming 3. Open houses 4. Floor duty 5. FSBOs 6. Expireds 7. Door-to-door and talking to neighbors

How many open houses did you have per month?	2.5 open houses per month
Was floor duty productive for you?	Overwhelming majority said yes
What was your average number of hours touring on tour day?	3.2 hours touring per tour day
Did you send [promotional] calendars?	Majority said yes
Did you wear your name tag on tour?	Majority said no
Did you agree to take other agents' business when they were out of town?	Overwhelming majority said yes
What did you do to learn neighborhoods?	(from highest rated to lowest rated): 1. Preview 2. Just drive 3. Tour 4. Computer 5. Open houses 6. Listening to other agents
Did any deal [collapse just before closing] in your first year?	1.5 deals average, vast majority FHA deals.
What was the least productive thing you tried your first year?	(from least to most productive): 1. Canvassing door-to-door 2. Cold calling 3. Mass mailings 4. Door hangers and apartment flyers 5. Open houses 6. Geofarming
Do you think agents should become accredited in anything their first year, such as Graduate REALTOR® Institute (GRI) or Accredited Buyer Representative (ABR)?	Majority said no
How many listings did you take your first 12 months?	8

What Etzenhouser learned from his survey was that most new agents, even the ones who proved successful, did not really have a good understanding of what the business was about when they started. In fact, he believes brokers who recruit new agents often tell them what a "natural" they are for real estate, but rarely tell them exactly what they need to do to be successful.

As a result, he has a developed a fast track for his new agents—rules, if you will—about activities he wants to see his agents partake in, beginning with their first week in the office.

Research a Single Neighborhood or Subdivision and Become an Expert in It

"I have them drive every street in that neighborhood and tour every home that is for sale," he said. "I have them research every home that had been sold in that neighborhood for the past year. Which addresses were sold, how much did they sell for?

"I have them drive the perimeter of the subdivision. What are the schools? Churches? Where is the shopping? How do you get to the major highways that take you downtown? I have them get on the Internet. Find out everything they can from the Internet. Get maps." Etzenhouser wants his agents to understand what makes a neighborhood unique—find something that makes it a good place to live. They need to develop a list of its top selling points. But they also need to find out what its drawbacks may be—"it's too close to the train tracks," or "I can hear trucks backing up at the nearby shopping mall"—and discuss with him and others in the office how they should respond when a buyer raises such objections.

In other words, Etzenhouser says, put on your "buyer hat" and shop the neighborhood the same way a buyer would.

Work with Other Agents

"In the first 30 days, I have the new agent go with another agent to an appraisal. They should go with [a different] agent to a house inspection. With another agent, go to a closing. Sit with another agent during a loan application."

Etzenhouser wants his new agents to see how the various elements of the transaction come together. But he also wants the
new associates to spend some time with experienced agents, talking about the business, selling styles, going beyond the company
classroom training to seeing how deals actually work on the
street.

Floor Duty

He assigns new sales agents to floor duty (floor time, call
time, whatever it's called in your office) so they start as soon as
possible talking to consumers about real estate issues and developing leads.

Help Hold Open Houses

"An open house has two purposes," he says. "You get to work
with an experienced agent and you get exposure to new buyers."
Throughout their early street training, Etzenhouser keeps close
tabs on the progress and activity of his new agents. "I follow up
with them. I schedule meetings with them to see what they are
doing. I have them bring their list of current prospects so we can
discuss each one. I expect them to have a deal on the board in
the first 45 days. I get a little worried if I don't see that happen."
His schedule for new agents?

- **Week 1:** "By the end of the first week, I want them to have
  previewed at least one subdivision. I expect them to have
  held at least one open house. I also expect them to have
  mailed out announcements to everyone on their contact list
  and started making phone follow-ups."
- **Week 2:** "I want them to open up their area a little. I want
  them to preview another couple of subdivisions and think
  about where they'd be interested in working. They should
  have gone on at least one broker's tour of listings by now.
  This week, I want to see them jump into a car with different
  agents, people they don't know. My attitude is, 'Last week
  you learned from Joe, this week I want you to learn from

Judy.' I may have them do some specific tasks for different agents: Work up CMAs [comparative market analyses] or something. Go out on a showing with another agent. I want them talking about real estate everywhere they go. I want them talking about real estate to the woman at McDonald's who gives them coffee. I want them to be positive and excited."

- **Week 3:** "They should be following up on leads from open houses. They should have had board duty a couple of times and should have some leads from that. Hopefully, their leads list [sphere of influence, plus new leads] is between 70 and 150 by now. I'd like to see them calling ten people on that list every day."

- **Week 4:** "By now they should have at least five buyer leads. I'd like to see them closing at least three of those buyers in the next 30 days." By the third or fourth week, Etzenhouser will sit down with his new agents and help cull through each agent's prospect list. "New agents have a hard time discerning hot buyers from cold prospects. I'm going to work with the agents to make sure they are working with people who are motivated to buy or sell. We're going to move those people to the top of the list, and other people further down."

One of the worst things he sees is new agents spending too much time with customers who aren't motivated—hoping that eventually something will happen that will make them buy a house. "Hope springs eternal in a lot of new agents," says Etzenhouser. "They're convinced this buyer is going to buy this week. That's why I want to know who they are working with. If nothing is happening, I want them to move on to someone who is motivated to buy."

Finding a Head Start

There are, of course, other systems and other methods geared to making new agents more productive as fast as possible. Some trainers point out that there is no reason for sales training to wait until a new agent is fully licensed. They like to see people who are motivated enough to learn how to sell before their first day on the job.

Those trainers argue, "Why not develop your sphere-of-influence list before you get your license? Why not start taking sales-training classes at night while you're still doing your old job during the day? As long as a person does not engage in a real estate activity (an activity for which a real estate license is required), there is nothing wrong with a person beginning to work on his or her career."

Students may, for instance, begin coming in and familiarizing themselves with the office computer system. They may develop their contact lists. They can start learning about neighborhoods and attending open houses.

Like Etzenhouser, many trainers believe new agents are of little value if they do not have "product knowledge"—meaning that they need to know the inventory of homes on the market.

The fastest way to the first transaction is an early start. Recognition of a few realities early on also improves the chances of success.

Those realities include the following:

- *Think buyers.* The truth is, it's a lot easier in the beginning to find buyers than it is to find sellers. If money is a problem, it's usually cheaper to work with buyers because you don't have to buy 'For Sale' signs or put ads in the paper.
- *Think friends and family.* Odds are your first transaction is going to be a member of your family or a close friend. Start by critically analyzing the names on your list and identifying which ones are most likely to be motivated buyers. Move those names to the top of your list.
- *Get sales training.* If your company doesn't offer training,

then find some somewhere. Anywhere. Find somebody who is going to teach you a method of selling and then commit to it long enough to let it work. There are a lot of systems out there that work. They've been tried and they work. But you have to let them work. At the end of three months, if you're not getting deals, you may have to ask yourself how motivated you are.

- *Get a day planner and use it.* It's important for new agents to know what they are going to be doing tomorrow morning. Set up an activity for tomorrow. Make an appointment that you have to keep, or schedule yourself to make ten phone calls to people in your sphere of influence. Make a plan and follow it. Once an activity is completed, check it off. A final thing that is suggested seems so minor that its importance is often overlooked—having your business cards printed. Business cards are a confidence builder. They tell friends, family, and strangers alike that you are in the real estate business, that you're glad to be there, and that you want their business.

M a r g e   K a n e ■

Being in the Right Place

Marge Kane, sales manager for the giant Edina Realty based in Minnesota, has just two rules she wants new agents to embrace from their first day in the office: "Be there and be interested."

"The faster you get to know the experienced agents, the faster you're going to break into the network, and the faster you're going to get business," she says.

Kane believes there is business to be had in a real estate office every day if a new agent is interested and active in pursuing it. "A lot of times, our most experienced agents are getting sign calls [potential buyers who have seen one of the top producer's 'For Sale' signs on a property and are calling in about the property]. If the agent is really busy, they are more than happy to give new agents the spillover."

As mentioned before, those same top producers may want someone else to hold an open house on one of their properties during the weekend. "It's a good place to start picking up business," says Kane. Kane also says agents need to have a business plan. She constantly is asking agents, "'What are you doing tonight? What are you doing tomorrow?' My job is to always encourage the sales agents. I want them to know I'm behind them."

In helping agents set goals for themselves, Kane suggests these targets:

- By the end of the first week, you should have observed two or three top producers.
- By the end of the second week, you should have conducted at least one open house and maybe two.
- By the fourth week, you should be working with clients of your own.

"I know companies that take new agents and send them straight to training classes from eight to five. I think that's insane. I want my people out there working while they're training. They need the practical application."

Chapter 6

It's Your Money

At first, the cash-flow direction is out

I nvariably, new real estate agents misjudge how much money they need to survive the early days of their careers, and those "early days" can be as long as eight or nine months. Having a few hundred dollars tucked away in the bank, as many students have, just isn't nearly enough. Even a wonderful spouse with a good job may not be enough to sustain your family while you're getting your career going. Remember, you're not just without income while you're building a career, you're investing in your business at the same time. More succinctly: No money is going to be coming in, but a lot of money is still going to be going out. If you talk to real estate office managers, top producers, or sales associates who have been in the business more than a year, you'll hear the same thing: They all wish they had stockpiled more cash before they began in real estate.

Just counting off the days on the calendar will tell you why. From the day you walk into the office, realistically and under the best of circumstances, it's going to be hard for you to get your first deal in the first 45 days. But let's be optimistic, let's say you do have your first closing in six weeks. You're not going to get your commission check at the closing table. In fact, depending on the office, it could be anywhere from another couple of weeks to a month before you actually have your share in your pocket.

That means, again under the best of circumstances, you won't have your first check until you've been in the business for a couple of months. That's a couple of months in the business without income (and with a lot of outgo, as you'll see in a moment) and that's just one check. If you're like most new sales associates, you have spent a lot of time focusing on your first deal. You may not know yet where your second deal is coming from.

The point is, until you get a steady flow of deals in the pipeline that produce a steady flow of checks to your bank account, you are not going to be at ease in the business.

How much do you realistically need to have set aside? First of all, of course, you just need basic living expenses: Money to pay your rent, to buy groceries, and gas money. Just money to live on. You can give yourself an idea of how much that is by figuring out how much you've spent in the past eight months.

Second, how much are you going to have to invest? As you already know, or should know, real estate is not a job where you can spend a thousand dollars or so on a business wardrobe and then take a bus to work everyday and collect your first paycheck in two weeks. Real estate is a career where you invest a thousand dollars or so in a business wardrobe (but keep reading, because you're going to be surprised at some of the attitudes about attire), plus you're going to spend a few hundred dollars on prelicense school, and probably a hundred dollars more just to take the exam and (assuming you pass it the first time) get your license.

That's money spent upfront just to give you the right to walk in the door of a real estate office and sit down at a desk. Now the real spending begins.

C u r t i s   H a l l ■

Plan for Pain, Spend for Success

Curtis Hall, a top producer for RE/MAX Anasazi Realty in Tempe, Arizona, warns new licensees that they simply cannot lose sight of what he calls "cost centers."

"You have to learn how to make the phone ring on a shoe-string budget. You can't lose sight of your budget. Ever. You think you're poor now [just starting out]. You haven't seen anything yet. For the next two years it's going to seem like all you ever do is write checks." Unfortunately, many real estate brokers, managers, and recruits don't talk to new licensees about the importance of budgeting and keeping close watch on how much is going out.

Hall, for instance, has been in the business about 12 years and is one of the top producers in his region. He sells between 60 and 75 houses each year, and his typical transaction is around $165,000.

Because today he works for RE/MAX, he keeps 100 percent of his split of the commission. (Many other real estate brokerages have followed the RE/MAX example and offer their top agents 100 percent.) But because he keeps his entire split, he also is obligated to pay for everything that he uses in his business. His office does not help him pay for anything and, in fact, charges him a "desk fee" in exchange for using its space and its name as a base for his business.

Itemizing Expenses

So how much does a top producer spend? "Let's just go down the list," he said.

Accountant. "I have to have an accountant. That was $832 last year. I need a pager so my clients know where to find me, that's $444. I lease a car for business, $3,910. Hotel room for my business plan, $1,400." Wait a minute. What did he mean by, "hotel for business plan"? "Every year I go somewhere and check into a hotel so that I can just think about my business. You can't just work in your business," he said. "You need to work *on* your business, too."

He escapes by himself to a distant city, holes up in a hotel room for a few days and just thinks. "I think about what I'm doing right in my business and what I'm doing wrong. I think about what I need to start doing, what I can expand on, and what I need to throw overboard. You can't just wander into this business one day and expect to be a success the next. It takes a plan of action and you need to spend time thinking about it and putting it together."

Conventions. "$3,000. You've got to go to conventions," he insisted. "You constantly need to be out there meeting people and hearing people talk about their business and how they are doing it, what's working for them and what isn't. You constantly need to expose yourself to new ideas. Anybody who says they don't have enough money to go to conventions, I say you'll never have any money if you don't go to conventions."

Dues. "$5,100." That seems like a high number, but, "I belong to a lot of things. They are a business expense. First of all, there's about $300 in [National Association of REALTORS®] dues. I belong to the Real Estate Educators Association [an organization of real estate speakers and instructors] and the Residential Sales Council [a REALTOR® group with advanced education in sales]. I belong to my state REALTOR® association and the local. I also belong to the Women's Council of REALTORS® [WCR], $198." The Women's Council? For a man? Says Hall, "Don't let the name fool you. And this is something new agents should know. One of the first things I did when I got my license was join the WCR. The truth is, women dominate this industry. Women are making a lot of money in this industry. Whether you are a man or a woman, if you want to be a success in this business, you need to associate with people who are successful. That's why I joined the Women's Council, and it's the smartest thing I ever did. I've learned more there than anywhere else. Worth every penny." Next expense?

Entertainment. "$7,000." That is a high number and certainly not one that new sales associates can expect to ring up for a while, but it does point up the fact that as you work with more buyers and sellers, your entertainment expenses are going to mount up. The most common example is when you have a buyer, and you are showing houses. You can't look at an endless stream of houses without taking a break? It may mean a coffee break in the morning, lunch in the afternoon, and maybe even a snack later. Remember: You're probably not going to be working with just one individual. Often, you'll have both the husband and wife in the car, and a lot of times you'll have their children, too.

So who pays for the donuts?

"I do," says Hall. "And sometimes you end up paying for lunch, too. But you'd be surprised at the number of times the clients will be buy you lunch . . . especially after you've gotten to know them pretty well. But I almost always buy the donuts."

Fixups. "Handy Andy, $3,700. 'Handy Andy' is a guy I hire to go out to the house and help the seller deal with minor problems before the house goes on the market. Or I might send him out to help the new buyer settle in. He'll do things like make sure the locks are changed and new keys are made up for the new owners. He might fix a light switch, put a new washer in a faucet. Nothing major. Just those nuisance things that a new owner doesn't want to bother with the day they move in." Some offices have their "Handy Andy" that they share. It's a good service to provide, and it's the kind of thing that helps you build your reputation as a service-oriented real estate agent.

Insurance. "Talk about something you wish your broker had told you," says Hall. "As soon as you go into the real estate business, your auto insurance is going to make a leap. If you're using your car for business and you're chauffeuring people around, your insurance is going to go up. Also, don't forget, you're probably not getting any benefits because you're an independent contractor. That means you have to pay for your own life insurance. Health insurance. If you're smart, you'll get disability insurance. Those can add up to some very big numbers." Again, ask around the office to learn what other agents are doing about those expenses. If you become a member of the National Association of REALTORS®, it has some programs available. Your company may have some kind of plan. But it is not at all unusual for you to bear the entire cost of your insurance needs. It comes with being an independent contractor.

Fees, Fees, Fees. "There are fees for the multiple-listing-system [where you advertise homes you have listed to other agents in the community. Some offices help defray that expense]. I have my own Web site, that's another $551 per year. Legal fees, $72. License renewal every two years [in his state], $125."

"Referral fees," he said, money you pay to real estate agents and organizations that send clients to you. "I paid out $38,912 in referral fees last year." (Be sure to read the material on referral fees at the end of this chapter.)

"Subscription fees to professional journals, $334. Computer expenses (laptop, desktop, and Palm), $10,600 per year. Fax machine, $224. You need a cell pone. Office supplies, $2,100. Continuing education—you think you just got out of school?— you're never out of school in real estate. There's another couple of hundred per course or seminar. Plus, you're going to need 'For Sale' signs, and you're going to need business cards."

Marketing. "Advertising. Doing what it takes to get the phone to ring with buyers and sellers on the other end, $34,243. The broker doesn't pay for any of that. That's all personal marketing. I've also hired a publicist ($11,300) who writes up press releases about me and organizes my advertising. New agents don't need anything like that to begin with. But I also spent more than $1,000 on postage. That's sending out postcards and letters just to keep my name in front of my sphere of influence."

Adding It up

Like many veteran agents, Hall has seen a number of new sales associates come into the business, think they are doing well, but then realize at the end of the year how little they actually are putting in their pockets.

"I can't tell you the number of young kids I see come in their first year. They work hard and things get going for them. Pretty soon they see they've made $100,000 in commissions their first year. But they don't budget. They don't watch every dime. They don't pay attention to what they're spending. Then they get hit with taxes. [Your broker doesn't take withholding out of your commission checks, like employers do in other jobs.] If you're not paying attention to what you're doing, you'll be out of the business in two years."

"Things your broker won't tell you? He won't tell you to save your money and not spend everything you make. I know 'top producers' who are years behind in paying their taxes. That's not what you want to have happen."

His advice: "New agents need to have a financial plan. They need to set aside—without fail—a percentage of every commission check, and it needs to go into some kind of retirement fund. If you look across this industry, I'd bet there isn't 1 in 10 agents who is saving money for the future."

A Little More about Referral Fees

Referral fees actually are somewhat controversial. As a new agent, you will likely be given an opportunity to participate—either individually or with your company—in networks of real estate agents that can spread around the world. Their purpose is simply to make sure that good clients who are transferred from a job in one location receive good service from a real estate agent on the other end of the move. Agents who take listings from people who are moving will help them sell their homes, but the agents also will forward those clients' names to your referral networks so the clients can be linked up with a quality agent on the other end to help them buy their next houses.

If the deal goes through, the agent on the receiving end pays a fee back to the network as a "thank you" for the business. If you are the referring agent, a portion of that fee will come back to you and your company for making the referral. If you are on the paying end of a referral fee, however, it can be pretty expensive. Depending on the network you belong to, you may end up paying 20 to 35 percent of your commission back to the network. Some agents complain that for all the work they need to do for the incoming client—long days of looking at homes, hours of preparation before the client even arrives, plus follow-up work to iron out problems—their share of the commission after the network takes its cut looks pretty thin.

It looks even thinner if you end up forgoing home-grown business to work with the out-of town-client.

New agents need to keep their pencils sharp and their calculators charged when considering any referral business. You need to make sure it's worth your time.

Chapter 7

Market Thyself—First

A whole lot of "dos" and surprisingly few "don'ts"

I t's a strange business, this real estate. It's not at all like any profession you've experienced before. At one moment you may be working with your colleagues against a competitor, and in the next moment you may be working with a competitor and shunning your colleagues. You never know who will bring the right buyer for a home you've got listed, and you never know who will list the perfect home for your next buyer. It could be the guy at the next desk. It could be someone you don't know in an office across town.

Want more irony? Sometimes you'll find your own company is your best friend, providing you training to put you on a pathway to success. Yet at other times, it will be studiously neutral about your career and whether you make any money at all.

Real estate is like no other job.

If you work at a grocery store, for instance, it doesn't matter who stocks the shelves or who handles the checkout lines. It doesn't matter who unloads the truck in the back or who helps carry bags out the front. If you do your job, and everyone else does his or her job, the company benefits—and if the company benefits, you benefit and the others around you benefit. Is teamwork necessary? You bet. And is there victory? Absolutely. Every time a shopper comes into your store instead of going to be another one, you win, your fellow workers win, and your company wins.

But not in real estate. In real estate you are, in fact, competing against everybody and, in one way or another, everybody is competing against you. Friendly competition, to be sure, but competition nevertheless. If the person at the next desk closes a big transaction, it's good for that person and good for the company, but it doesn't mean a thing to your paycheck. And if he closes a dozen great transactions, it's even greater for the company—but it still doesn't mean a thing to your paycheck. Your office may be selling more houses than it ever has before, but if *you're* not selling houses, it could be the worst year of your life. For you to move to the celebration side of the office, you need to promote yourself.

You need to make sure your name is known among the customers you want to serve. You want to make sure they know that when they need a real estate transaction, they should come to you. In fact, you want your name to be better known than your company's name. The concept is as clear as this:

If somebody calls your office just blindly looking for help, anybody with a license can help them, including the guy you don't like two desks over.

Your goal needs to be that you want people to call the office and ask for you by name. For that to happen, it means you have to promote yourself. You have to turn yourself into your own brand name, just like Coca-Cola or IBM.

J u l i e   A l i b r a n d o ■

Aggressive Self-Promotion

Explains top producer Julie Alibrando, "My name always goes with me. The name of the company I'm with may change, but my name is always the same and I always make sure my past clients know where I am." Like many new sales associates, when she first got into the business Alibrando thought the enthusiasm with which she was recruited would carry over into sales support after she got her license. And like many other new licensees, she was disappointed.

"As I look back on it, I don't think they really wanted me, 'Julie Alibrando.' What they really wanted was the people I knew. And I knew a lot of people. I think their hope was that those people would automatically come to me for real estate, and they'd benefit from it." That didn't happen. Although now a top producer with RE/MAX Preferred in Reedsburg, Wisconsin, a relatively small community, her first few years in the business were dreadful. On her first day of work she was simply shown her desk. "I was with my first company for two years. My second year, I only grossed $12,000. It was terrible," she concedes. Determined not to fail, however, Alibrando figured out she needed to get some education in salesmanship—something other than how to push buttons on a telephone. The first thing she did was call her local REALTOR® association to find out what courses were being offered and how much they'd cost. The REALTOR® board offered a four-day quick-start course that at least gave her some of the basics of the industry: It taught her about calling For Sale by Owner properties and how to make cold calls. "It was better than nothing, but it really didn't give me what I needed," she says.

What it did do, however, was acquaint her with a REALTOR® affiliate organization, the Certified Residential Specialists. "I immediately started taking CRS classes [and at the same time she was earning her Graduate, REALTORS® Institute designation] and it's one of the smartest things I've ever done. The cost was somewhere between $200 and $250 per course."

The courses weren't offered in her hometown, however, so she had to travel to a larger city, which meant staying in a hotel. The entire cost was borne by her, more than $800. Her company did not pick up the tab.

Although she was learning more techniques, implementing them in her office was a different problem. "I'm not a good person at asking for help. I'm very independent. I would sometimes ask my broker for help, 'What should I do about this?' or 'How do you handle that?' Usually I didn't get a lot of help. Most of the time I had to figure out things on my own." Nor did her fellow agents in the office provide much help. "You really can't get a lot of information from another agent. You're in competition with them. They aren't going to give you their secrets." Learning from CRS national instructors, however, Alibrando began breaking the mold. And one of the first things she did was start marketing herself.

"I was the first real estate agent in my town to run my picture in an ad in the newspaper. It said, 'Remember Julie.' Nobody had ever done that before. The other agents in town laughed and said it wouldn't work, but I kept doing it, every week. It was always something short like, 'Need to sell your house? Remember Julie.' And my picture and my phone number. I usually didn't even put in my last name 'cause nobody could pronounce it anyway.

"I was also the first agent in town to put my picture on my business card. I learned that from the CRS classes. I was marketing *me* because I didn't have any listing to market. Nobody else in town was doing personal promotion." The owner of the company frowned on Alibrando's dare-to-be-different attitude. "Everybody in the office had the same business card. The same colors, the same logo. Only the names were different. I changed my business card and put my picture on it. I showed it to my broker and she didn't say anything. She scrunched up her nose and that was it." In pursuit of her marketing strategy, Alibrando made sure every piece of marketing material she distributed carried the same message, along with her picture.

"You have to decide you don't care what anybody else says. If you've got an idea to market yourself that you think will work, you do it. Forget the idea that your broker is going to do anything for you. Most brokers aren't going to help with personal promotion. I just figured that because it was my business, I had to take it upon myself to make it grow." Even though she wasn't in management, Alibrando went ahead and got her broker's license because she felt consumers held brokers in higher regard than they held "agents." "I had some snide comments [from other agents] and people told me I was wasting my money. But I kept doing it."

In fact, just about the only people who were buying into her personal promotion were consumers who wanted to buy or sell houses. "And you know something, nobody ever asked me how long I had been in the business. No one ever asked me what my experience was." She tells the story of when, in her first year in business, she had to go head-to-head with an experienced agent who was the dominating lister in an area she wanted to farm. The veteran agent told the seller, "Julie doesn't really have much experience. I do. And she really hasn't been around this area that long. I have." The seller responded to the agent, "Well, how is she going to get the experience if nobody ever hires her?" Alibrando got the listing.

"I had the impression that brokers in town laughed at me, but people saw that I was being aggressive—a least a heck of lot more aggressive than any of the other agents were being. People liked that."

Feeling she was getting nowhere with her first company, Alibrando moved to another office—RE/MAX—where the supervising broker urged her to continue doing what she was doing. She accelerated her "Julie Sells" campaign, and her income grew accordingly.

She also was the first in her real estate community to invest in a personalized Web site, www.juliesells.com. "My first Web site was ugly. But it was out there and nobody else was. I think it cost me about $180 for two years. It was gross."

But far and away the greatest piece of personal promotion Alibrando has is the one she drives. She loves the color purple, and her business car is a big purple Chevy Blazer.

"I drive that thing all over town, all around the lake area [where she does a lot of work]. People know it's me. 'There goes Julie in her purple Blazer.' It has a RE/MAX sign on the side with my name on it. They keep telling you, 'Don't be a secret agent.' You have to let people know you're in the business. Don't be embarrassed to put your name out there."

That purple Blazer represents a sales lesson for every new associate:

When Alibrando decided she wanted to carve out a place for herself selling lake properties, she had to take business away from the established professional who had worked the area for years—

the same one who tried to convince sellers not to choose Julie because of her lack of experience.

"I just started cruising around the lake. People would see me constantly coming and going in that purple Blazer. They thought I was showing houses. But in the beginning, I was just driving around out there every chance I could. I'd stop. I'd meet people. Talk to them about what was going on around the lake. Twice a month I gave them updates on what houses were selling for."

She did follow-up mailings and made personal contact whenever possible. "I'm now the top selling agent in the lakes areas," Alibrando say. "It happened because the guy who was the top agent didn't work as hard as I did. He was complacent. He thought the business would just naturally come to him.

"The truth is, people forgot about him. He may have sold them a house eight years ago, but he didn't keep in touch with them. They forgot about him. Just because someone has been in the business for years, don't think you can't work into his area. You can."

Chapter 8

Do You Know Where You're Going?

I wish I had realized earlier how much control I had over the direction of my career

From death by cold calling to success as an urban consultant: the story of Edward Krigsman is a story that shows how having the direction you want for your career is the way to success.

Edward Krigsman ■

Taking Control of Your Career

It's 6 o'clock on an early summer evening in Seattle, and Edward Krigsman is in the office, trying to get out to a "business seminar." When he does get there he'll learn about competition and management. And flexibility. He'll learn about how to press an advantage, and what it takes to win—the importance of thinking on your feet and the ability to make instant decisions where results are immediate. But Krigsman, a top producer at John L. Scott Real Estate Inc., is not heading out to some hotel ballroom and he doesn't have tickets to hear some grand master of salesmanship. He's trying to get to Safeco Field to watch the Seattle Mariners play baseball. Business management at its best.

"I'm not really a sports fan," he says. "But it's inspiring to me to watch the Mariners . . . to watch how Piniella manages the team . . . to watch Ichiro decide to steal a base. You can learn a lot about real estate by studying other things, other successful organizations, like good sports teams, and watching how they compete."

When the Mariners lost their "top producers" a couple of years ago—Ken Griffey, Jr., to the Cincinnati Reds and Alex Rodriguez to the Texas Rangers—everybody expected the team to crash. Instead, "It's a better team than it ever was. You're seeing people push their skills further than they thought they could. And you see coaches working with the players to get everything they can. This is real competition. It's a lot like real estate. It's a game and it's fun. It's competition and competition is fun."

That "competition is fun" philosophy has taken Krigsman from desperate times just a few years ago to the top of Seattle's inner-urban real estate market today. He does some $15 million in volume per year working condos, single family homes, and a little new construction: Just about everything is priced between $225,000 and $600,000. And although he seems like a likely candidate for success in some profession, he doesn't necessarily seem like a likely candidate for success in real estate.

He's only been in the business since 1998. He had no obvious niche when he started out. And in a business built on the words "location, location, location," Krigsman couldn't have gotten a job as cab driver—literally. "I had lived in Seattle when I was young but I had moved away. The city had changed a lot while I was gone. I didn't really know anybody. I had to get used to it all over again."

What Krigsman did have, however, was an instinct for success, a notion of how to move in the right direction, and the ability to listen to those who could help and ignore those who couldn't. "When I started out there were a lot of naysayers. A lot of people said I wouldn't make it. It was a hard life. I didn't have any experience [as a real estate agent]. They asked why I wanted to be in a business where the people really weren't very well respected. They said I was overqualified and overeducated to be a real estate agent." And, he concedes, for a while it appeared the naysayers were right. For his first seven months in real estate in

Seattle, Krigsman, who had owned an architectural restoration business in Chicago, made no money. Not "no money to speak of." He made no money at all. He was making an hour and half commute to downtown daily from his parents' home in the suburbs. He finally ended up renting the cheapest studio apartment he could find so he could be closer to work.

"It was terrible. I wasn't doing any business. I really didn't have any leads. I went to my broker and told her I was going to have to quit. It wasn't working. I wasn't making any money. And I didn't think I was ever going to."

His broker, however, responded with patience and confidence, and urged him to have the same.

"She had a lot of faith in me. She felt I could be successful in real estate. She said she'd loan me money so I wouldn't have to quit. That's how confident she was."

Her confidence paid off. Within the next six months Krigsman was selling enough homes that he felt he could make a living. Within a few months after that, he began realizing he could actually make a lot of money in real estate. By the end of his third year in the business, he saw no reason why he couldn't be one of the community's top producers. But, he recalls, the early days were tough.

Career-Killing Cold Calls

When he first came into the business, his company embraced the theory that cold calling was the shortest path to an agent's first transaction. For Krigsman it was deadly.

"I hated it. Make 100 cold calls a day, every day. I did that for months. I got no business from it. I got very few leads. It just wasn't what I wanted to do. In hindsight, there may have been some value to it. But mostly, I'd have to say I wasted a lot of time." There were other "programs" as well. "I tried a lot of different things. Nothing worked. It was really frustrating." Eventually, however, Krigsman realized that what he needed was a niche to call his own. Other agents were working their farms—their neighborhoods and their social circles—but being an outsider, Krigsman seemed to have no automatic "ins."

Then it occurred to him that maybe being an outsider was his "in." "I didn't know anybody, which was really bad because this is a relationship business. It made for a fascinating time, trying to bootstrap a business without any contacts. But I figured out I could focus my client base on recent arrivals to the Seattle area. Other people just like me. It was the only way I could level the playing field [against agents working established farms].

"I saw a lot of people who were in the same situation I was. Young people moving to Seattle. A lot of them taking jobs in the technology sector. They didn't know very many people and they didn't know the city very well. So we had things in common."

As a graduate of the Ivy League's Brown University in Providence, Rhode Island, Krigsman was entitled to membership in the Brown University Club of Seattle. "I started meeting other Brown graduates. And that started generating a little business."

He also began holding open houses for other agents in his office. "I was starting to come in contact with people whom I had a lot in common with. Those leads would lead to ten referrals. They were mostly young people from somewhere else. They were techno-savvy [as is Krigsman]. We connected."

One of the chief points of connection, Krigsman found, was a near universal dislike of the stereotypical real estate salesman. Young homebuyers had a fear of being hustled and didn't want to waste time with someone trying to sell them something they didn't want. Ironically, that fit Krigsman just fine. "I don't like salesmen, either. I position myself as a consultant, not a salesman. My clients know that and they appreciate it." (He concedes, however, that he has since deepened his "appreciation of what commissioned salespeople go through.")

Offering himself as a consultant continues to serve him well. "Consumers are overloaded with information [because of the Internet]. What they need is someone to help analyze it. Help them understand it. I deal with a lot of highly educated people. They understand the Internet and they know how to use it. In the old days, real estate agents used to tell their clients about new listings. Now the clients are telling the real estate agents when there's something new. They have access to the information. My job is to help them understand that information."

Like other successful agents, Krigsman does have a Web presence, but he candidly admits it does very little to actually put money in his pocket.

"A Web site gives me credibility with my sellers," he says. "It doesn't bring me a lot of [buyer] leads. But my sellers want to know it's there."

What It Takes to Survive

In retrospect, Krigsman believes a couple of factors have helped build his success.

First, he says, "I've never had a real job. I've always worked for myself." People who cannot go out and generate business on their own are unlikely to do well in real estate over the long term.

Second, "It's important that you know who you are." Krigsman has lived all over the world, but always in an inner-city setting. He does his best work with other city dwellers. "Work with clients you enjoy working with."

Third, "Develop a lot of mentors. Not just people in your company, but people who are outside the industry. Every time I've had a major jump in market share, I had talked to one of my mentors first. You see what's working in another business, and you adapt it to your own." And inside the business? "Study people who are successful. Seek them out. They are willing to share information."

Fourth, "Take time to understand a little about your customer's business. They appreciate someone who knows about their products or tools. It's important."

Fifth, "Don't have unrealistic expectations. Don't think you can be successful without working."

Finally, if—and when—a deal caves in, "Move on." "Don't harp on past failures," Krigsman says. "Sometimes it's not even worthwhile to understand why things fell apart. There is an expression we use in my office when a deal falls apart, it's 'NEXXXTTTTTT!!!!!'" And what does Krigsman wish his broker had told him? "She probably told me and I probably didn't listen, but you really are on your own."

Chapter 9

Family Matters

If you ignore them, they will go away

So let's be realistic. Do families and a real estate career mix? Can you get to where you want to go professionally without sacrificing personally? As always, there are no clear-cut answers. But in this case, an honest and realistic response has to be this: It's a struggle. There are going to be sacrifices, especially as you start out. You are going to find yourself trading off family time for real estate time. You are going to miss some soccer practices. You are going to be late to some gymnastics meets. You are going to find yourself answering the phone at night and getting into the car to go meet a client, when you'd much rather be at home. And, of course, the younger your children are, the more difficult it's going to be.

Does it get better? Sure. Two obvious things happen: You get more experience and you start making more money, meaning you start taking control of your own life and the children get older and understand a little better why you need to work.

Jan Millsaps ■
Life's Little Priorities

Jan Millsaps, a sales associate for Craven & Co. REALTORS® in Concord, North Carolina, has three boys, a husband, and a career—and not always in that order. Her two older boys, 9 and 7, go to school, her youngest, 4, goes to half-day preschool from 9 to 12. Those hours pretty well define her business day.

"Right now my 9-year-old will still throw a temper tantrum. It's a pretty good sign he needs more Mom time," she says. "But he's pretty good with me having to work a lot."

"I schedule closings and appointments during those times," she says. Her youngest child stays with a friend all day on Tuesdays, which means she can go to the office sales meeting and extend her business day into the afternoon. Her husband, a teacher at a private high school, is usually available after 3:30 in the afternoon.

An active real estate career can mean fewer home-cooked meals and, while it is important that the family eats together, dinner often doesn't come until 7 or 7:30 in the evening. She is not yet at the point in her career, however, where she no longer has to take "call time"—calls that come into the office and are routed back out to an agent on call. "The only time I'm obligated to be in the office is Tuesday morning [sales meeting]. Other than that, I work out of my home."

And what happens when a call comes to the house and her youngest is at home, and the client wants to go see a property? "The first thing I do is ask if we can schedule the appointment the next morning when I have child care, or maybe later on another afternoon when I can get help. But if I can't work it out, I take him with me. I explain to the client that I'm a working mother. A lot of the time they have children too, so they don't see it as a problem."

She will not, however, take her 4-year-old to show an owner-occupied house. "He's at the age where he thinks everything is a toy. He's into everything, so I can't take him on those showings."

Taking her son while she's doing business does make her feel less professional, she says, but she's never gotten a complaint from a client. And, she says, her broker has never raised the issue either. "He isn't concerned. As long as I'm producing, as long as I'm making money, he doesn't care."

In fact, it was her broker, back when she was starting out and trying to balance children, husband, and career, who urged her to take more control of her life. "A call would come in and I'd drop everything to go out and show a house. My broker told me that if people are impulsive and can't wait until tomorrow, they're not going to buy. And he was right. Now I just suggest some alternative times. I'll work with them to find time, but I don't drop everything anymore.

"My broker lectured me about how it was 'my life,' and I had to take more control of it. And I have taken more control."

Millsaps estimates she spends about 10 hours per week in her office and about 40 hours per week total in some kind of real estate–related endeavor. "I don't work 60-hour weeks anymore," she said. There have been sacrifices. She feels confident she could make more money if she could focus on her career. "I think I'd be one of the top producers." And there are plenty of things she no longer has time for—such as coffee with other moms. "Time is spent either working or at home," she says.

But she does manage to remain active in her church, and she spends at least two hours per day on the Internet, responding to e-mail and marketing herself. Half of her business, she says, has evolved from contacts made at church or by volunteering at her husband's school. "The important thing is to set your priorities and stick to them," she says. She even has her business hours on her business card.

Still, "I couldn't do it if I didn't have a wonderful husband who is willing to pull more than his share of the work. Thanks to him, it just all fell into place."

Heather Littrell ■

Balancing for Fun and Profit

Another working mother at the Craven & Co. office is Heather Littrell, who has a 7-year-old ballerina for a daughter and a 2-year-old son. She has been in the business for nine years—beginning before she had children—and has found that children do add a challenge to the job. "I pretty much work 9 to 5 now," she says. "I've pretty much found that if you're good at what you do, people will wait for you." She no longer does showings at night or on weekends, but acknowledges she did when she began her career in the early '90s.

"Initially, I did pretty lengthy interviews with all my [buyers] first. But now I don't do so much of that. I send them to a lender to do the financial interviewing. It's a lot more efficient."

Littrell's career now is at a place where she can rely on repeat business and referrals—and car pooling for the kids with other mothers. "I've found that people are flexible and you can usually work things out if they are sincerely interested."

"On Sundays, I tell some people I'm home with my family and I can't leave for business. They usually say that's fine. The general public thinks we can make our own hours anyway. They think it's the perfect job, that we can work around our children." That's a misconception, but one that works in favor of the industry.

Littrell believes life would be easier for her if she had extended family nearby to help with the children during work hours. Instead, she relies on a licensed assistant to help on the business side of her life.

"If I was talking to brand-new agents about working and having a family, the first thing I'd tell them is to hook up with another agent so you can cover for each other. If you're out of town, the other agent can take a showing for you. You can write up the contract when you get back. If it's something urgent and the contract has to be written up right away, the other agent can write it and you can reimburse him or her for the time."

Like Millsaps, Littrell believes that staying active with her children has improved her business.

"I'd say about 20 percent of my business comes from families I've met by working in my children's classrooms. My daughter is in gymnastics and ballet. I volunteer at school. People get to know what business you're in."

Hugh Ryall ■

There's Always Room at the Bottom

South Carolina instructor Hugh Ryall argues that few managing brokers prepare their new agents for the kind of rigors they can expect in the business. "If you're not careful, real estate will consume you. You see young agents, and they are so hungry for business, they're going 24 hours a day, 7 days a week. If the phone rings at 11 at night, they're off to show a home."

The sooner new agents learn professional discipline, he says, the better off they'll be—and that means setting a normal work schedule, setting time for family activities, and most of all, "not allowing that time to be disturbed." "You're a professional, just like other professionals," he says. "People don't call their attorneys at 11 o'clock at night and expect them to go do something. They don't call their CPAs at 7 A.M. and expect them to drop what they're doing."

Ryall teaches a course entitled "There's Always Room at the Bottom," where agents are taught how to take control of their own lives. "Brokers won't tell these new agents that they need to set up a business plan and write a mission statement. They just hand them the listing book and say, 'Now go sell your aunt and uncle a house.'"

The mission statement should include what the new agent hopes to get out of his or her real estate career and the business plan sets out a method to achieve it. "In your business plan, you need to set up a budget. You need to know how much money you need and where you hope it comes from. You need to set your priorities, and your family needs to be among those priorities."

In some cases, Ryall says, that means scheduling appointments for family events just the same as you make appointments to show houses. You wouldn't miss a showing, so you shouldn't miss a family event.

"If you don't do it," Ryall says, "This business will cannibalize you. But if you look around, there are plenty of agents working four-and-half or five days a week, taking weekends off, and they are doing quite well. You see so many new agents running around helter-skelter. The only thing they know is that they're working hard to get business. Just because they are working hard doesn't mean they are doing the right things. Real estate is a fascinating, rewarding career if you don't let it overtake you."

Chapter 10

Working With Friends and Family

It's a little like how you all get along during the holidays

Memorize this chapter, then rip it out of the book. Then burn it and scatter the ashes. Do it at night so no one sees you. And don't tell anyone I told you to do it. It's time to discuss the dark side of real estate—what really happens when you work with friends and family.

The Ties That Bind

It is true that one of the first things you'll do in real estate is create a sphere-of-influence list of people you've known most of your life. The list will comprise your friends and family members and probably your neighbors, too. These are the people you'll be sending postcards to that announce your entry into the business, and you'll be following up with a phone call to many of them, making sure they got your card and that they put it right there on the refrigerator. You want to make sure, again, that they understand that you're a real estate agent now and that means you can help them buy or sell a house. Don't be bashful about spelling it out. It is from this list, most likely, that your first deal will come.

Now, let it first be said that with any luck, your friends and family will be supportive of your new efforts in the real estate business. It's doubtful that any of them actually want you to fail. But it's also fair to say that some of them, when they heard you were going into real estate, probably rolled their eyes—still not sure what was wrong with the last career you had and wondering how long you'll stick with this one. Hopefully, most of that conversation will take place behind your back and out of earshot.

The Challenge of Business and Relationships

Of course, sometimes friends aren't as friendly as they could be. Let's face it, we may be talking about the same people who were giving you wedgies in Middle School or competing with you for prom dates in High School. It's going to be hard for them to make a distinction between the person you were then and the person you've become now. It's going to be hard for them to take you completely seriously. In some cases, it is going to be very hard for you to convert a family or friend relationship to a business relationship.

For instance, consider your Aunt Gertrude. Perhaps she's at an age where she might be thinking about downsizing her living space. And now that you are thinking about it, is Cousin Laurie going to need to make a change now that the divorce is final? And what about your nephew James? He really shouldn't be living with his mother and father anymore. And didn't your neighbor's niece just get engaged? They'll need a house.

Many times you are going to find that family members just don't understand how your business works. You may have just joined a real estate office with roots in the community, but then see that a family member has listed her home with a national franchise, thinking she'd get better exposure. It's your job to make sure people understand that, thanks to the Internet, your company could expose their property to buyers around town, around the country, or around the world.

Alternatively, you may have just joined a major national franchise, only to have a friend list with a corner realty shop. Explanation? "I thought you guys just did national deals." Again, you've failed to make clear that real estate is a local business and that you live and work in the same community your friend does.

Coulda, Woulda, Shoulda

You could easily have handled either of those deals, but for all practical purposes they were gone before you got to them. A little more effort to educate your friends and family might have saved the deals, but it also might not have. These things happen.

As you're starting out, you'll hear a lot of explanations for why you didn't get a friend or family member's business:

- "I decided not to use you until you had a little more experience." (They've forgotten that your entire company and a veteran supervisor are backing you up on everything you do.)
- "I would have used you, but I really needed this deal done right." (But they'll call you the next time they need a deal done wrong?)
- "I considered using you, but I thought someone else could get me a higher price." (Owners only *think* they set the price of their house. In reality, the market sets the price.)
- "I really wanted a more professional relationship with a real estate agent." (Of course, every other agent in town is trying to develop a "friendship" relationship with him.)
- And from homebuying relatives: "I don't want you to see how much money I make." (Or how much they're in debt).

These are all excuses that are difficult, if not impossible, to deal with, and they are going to leave you kicking walls and screaming into pillows. Maybe if you had educated them a little better, or gotten to them a little sooner, it might have made a difference. But it also might not have. Even top sales trainers who tour the country with their seminars say you can't manage family the way you manage a business. Logic just doesn't work.

On the other hand, sometimes the deals that do come to you from friends and family can be just as frustrating:

- "I wanted to list with you because I didn't want to tell any-body about the leaky basement." (Property defect disclosure is a matter of law in almost every state and it's illegal to con-spire with sellers—even if they're family.)
- "Oh, by the way, your Mom said you'd cut your commission for me." (Ah, the family discount.)
- "I'm using you because I just know you'll be sure to get, well, you know, the 'right sort' of people to buy this house. I would never want to sell to any [fill in the blank with your favorite ethnic group]." (Sorry, Aunt Sally, but fair housing is, well, you know, "a law.")

J e f f   N e l s o n ■

Preventing Commissiondectomies

In the past 25 years, Jeff Nelson, a veteran broker-owner of Hastings, Johnson & Nelson in Sioux Falls, South Dakota, has probably heard almost every excuse there is for why people are going to want you to cut your commission. He's also trained thou-sands of agents in how to talk to people about matters of price.

"When you're a new agent, and someone asks you to cut your commission, the first thing you say is 'no.' Commissions are set by company policy," he explains. "As a brand-new real estate agent, you don't have the latitude to cut the commission. The best thing to do is explain to them that you don't have the authority to cut the commission, but if they'd like to talk to your broker they can go ahead and call him. They never call. But the point is that it takes you [the new agent] out of the loop."

Sales-training schools typically include sections on how to defend your commission against those who think you should take a little less. Often trainers will suggest that agents say things such as, "No, I won't cut my commission. If I can't protect my own compensation, how would I ever protect your sales price?"

Other trainers recommend simply trying to explain how much you, as an agent, make in a deal. Using the theoretical sale of a $100,000 home, they suggest that you explain that half of a 6 percent commission—amounting to $3,000—goes to the agent who brought the buyer, leaving you with $3,000. You then need to point out that half of your $3,000 goes to the company, leaving you with just $1,500—money you use to help advertise the house, send out flyers, put up the For Sale sign, and pay for other incidentals before you put anything in your pocket.

"When people see how much the agent actually makes, they usually drop the request to cut the commission," Nelson says. Other sales trainers say that if you are asked to cut your commission, you should take six $1 bills out of your wallet and lay them side-by-side, then essentially make the same explanation as above. Take away three of the bills, representing the other agent's share of the commission. Then take away another bill, and fold one of the two remaining bills in half, representing how much goes to the company. The remainder, you explain, is for your expenses and for you to live on. You have to pay your taxes out of that, all your Social Security deductions, and your insurance. You remind people that as an independent contractor, your company does not contribute benefits the way other companies do.

Says Nelson, "Most people will say, 'Oh, I never thought of it that way.' They'll never bring the subject up again." But, he adds, some people will persist, suggesting that, "I've talked to three other agents and they all say they'll cut the commission."

The answer here is tougher. "I just have my agents explain, 'Those other agents may have smaller advertising budgets or they can just get along on less. I know I can't do it for less. But I can guarantee that I'll still be here in 30 or 60 or 90 days, and those other agents may be out looking for jobs by then.'"

Nelson points out that as you gain more experience in the business, you will be given more flexibility to change the commission structure of a deal. But in all cases, the deal has to be driven by "what makes sense" for everyone involved, including you. Many sellers won't know and won't care what your expenses are. They are only trying to get by as cheaply as they can.

"I have seen cases where a seller will ask an agent to cut his commission, and the agent will make him a counteroffer," Nelson said. "The agent will say that he'll cut his portion of the commission by a third—from 3 percent to 2 percent—if the seller is willing to cut a third of his equity and reduce the asking price by that much. If a seller has $30,000 in equity, the agent asks the seller to cut a third of that—$10,000—off the asking price. The agent explains that if the seller is willing to take $10,000 less, the house will sell a lot faster and the agent won't have to do nearly as much advertising to get it sold, so he doesn't mind reducing his commission." Nelson says, however, that agents have to do their homework before they make such an offer and need to be sure their sellers have substantial equity. "If the guy is upside down on the house [if the house has deteriorated in price to less than what he bought it for], it could backfire on you."

Everything, says Nelson, comes down to confidence for new agents, and usually family members can be counted on to help. "You know, most of the time friends and family members are very supportive. They want you to be a success, and they want to help you get the experience you need. Most of them know it's a tough business and they're willing to back you."

Additional thought: There is a lot of confusion about where real estate commissions come from. Some people think they are set by law or by the state's real estate regulators. They're not. Other people think they are set by the local Board of REALTORS®. They're not. (In fact, many people think the local Board of REALTORS® is a government entity. It's not.)

The truth is that real estate commissions are set the same way any other price is set on any other service or commodity: After an evaluation of what it costs to produce a service, and after an evaluation of what competitors are charging for the same service, the broker-owner will determine how much he wants to charge, including a profit margin for himself.

Although newspapers and magazines like to say, "Real estate commissions are negotiable," the reality is they may or may not be. Commissions are set as a matter of individual company policy. That policy may have some flexibility built into it, or it may not. Talk to your supervising broker.

Chapter 11

Competitors and Predators and You

Kind of fun once you get the hang of it

I n California, not that long ago, two agents from the same company—each with a competing buyer—were making bids to buy the same house. At the time, the real estate market was raging in the state and housing was in tight supply. Buyers were desperate. Sellers could expect two, three, four, or even more buyers to bid for their homes. Prices were soaring, and sellers were making outrageous profits. Not only were houses being sold *above* their listing prices, but in some cases for *double* their listing prices. Competition between agents was fierce. This was no place for bashful real estate agents.

For this particular house, the bidding had been furious, and during the course of offers and counteroffers, several would-be buyers already had dropped out. Finally, the only two buyers left happened to be represented by agents from the same office. When at last it appeared the bidding had gone as far as it would go, and a very high price had been extracted by the sellers and their agent, the sellers finally verbally agreed to accept the highest bid. On the basis of that verbal OK and handshakes all around, the "winning" real estate agent stepped out of the room for a moment to call her buyers on her cell phone. All she needed was a confirmation on the final price and terms and, of course, to congratulate them on winning the house. While the winning agent was out of the room, however, the opposing agent representing the losing buyers came back in, pulled a new and higher bid from her pocket, and insisted the sellers reopen negotiations. In the time it took the first agent to make a cell-phone call, the sellers changed their minds, reopened the process and ultimately accepted the bid from the "losing" agent—an incredible turn of events.

Moral of the story: *You are in business for yourself.* You would like to believe that in this story, extraordinary times and the extraordinary market forced the real estate agents in this case to behave in an extraordinary fashion. To some degree, that is probably true. But even as a new agent working in much calmer markets, you have to be ready for fierce competition to break out. If you have a buyer who sees a house he or she absolutely must have and another agent has another buyer who feels exactly the same way, you could suddenly find yourself in the middle of heated negotiations with a seller and against even an officemate.

One of the things you won't learn in prelicense school is *guile.* You won't learn how to be clever or artful. You won't learn how to get around seemingly huge obstacles (like a higher bid). This is another demonstration of why sales-training schools and seminars are an absolute must for any real estate agent just as soon as—or even before—he or she actually goes to work. This is another reason why you need to befriend the top producers in your office. Like any trade, there are some tricks worth knowing. In the course of your career, you are likely to be on the right side of some of these strategies. Sometimes, of course, you might find yourself on the wrong side, too.

A l a n   B i g e l o w ■

Knowmanship

Alan **Bigelow of** Coldwell Banker Chicagoland is both a prelicense instructor and sales trainer who travels the country helping sales associates sharpen their skills. He describes new sales associates just coming out of schools as "licensed to kill. Their biggest problem is they don't know what they don't know."

In his "Fast Start" training classes that he conducts for Coldwell Banker, he explains to brand-new sales associates that there are only four ways to make money in real estate:

1. *Listing property*: "That's getting the seller to sign a piece of paper that says he'll pay you to sell his house."
2. *Selling property*: "That's putting the buyer in the back seat and driving him around town."
3. *Referrals*: "I explain to them that if someone they know is moving to another area, they can refer that buyer to another agent and get a fee in return."
4. *Recruiting*: "Some offices pay a recruiting bonus if you recruit someone else to join the company."

But he underscores that the primary source of income for sales associates is listing and selling houses. "We work on dialogues. I'll sit a new agent down and we'll role-play. Agents hate it. But if they can convince me they'll do a good job selling my house, then they should be able to convince a seller."

Such rehearsing also is important when questions of commission—or, more specifically, cutting the commission—come up from the seller. "I am known to be very tough on commissions," says Bigelow. "I think the real issue is, 'Who has the greater loss?'" Bigelow explains that it's not unusual for a home to go on the market for $300,000 and have a buyer respond in the neighborhood of $290,000. Negotiations may get the seller down to $295,000 and the buyer up to $293,000. "Then the seller or the buyer looks at you and asks whether you'll cut your commission to make the deal happen. I say 'no.' The real question [sales associates] need to answer here is, 'Who has the most to lose?' If the seller doesn't take the offer, he loses a $293,000 sale. It's probably costing him 1 percent per month [in mortgage, insurance, maintenance expenses, etc.] to continue to pay for a house he doesn't want to live in anymore. He needs to figure out what it's costing him to turn down the buyer's offer."

And on the buyer's side? "If the buyer doesn't come up with a higher price, he risks losing the home of his choice. He has to start all over again." Bigelow, of course, stands to lose his commission. On a $295,000 sale, the total commission may work out to be about $18,000, half of which goes to the other agent in the deal, with Bigelow sharing the remaining portion with his company. "I don't see how I have the greatest loss if the deal doesn't happen."

The Importance of People-Watching

Bigelow believes that one of the most important things an agent working with a buyer must figure out first is, "Who is going to buy the house?" In every deal, he says, a dominant personality emerges who will decide whether to purchase the home.

"You think in a perfect world that the husband and wife will split the decision 50/50. The reality is it's always 51/49. One is always stronger than the other." Bigelow says body language and conversation between husband and wife will usually tell which one will "buy" the house. Once the sales agent knows who is in charge of the decision making, finding and buying the right home will go more smoothly.

He also urges his new sales associates to learn to move as quickly as possible toward a personal relationship with the buyer or seller. On the buyer side, the hope is that it's harder to be disloyal to a friend than to a business acquaintance. On the seller side, a friendly relationship now could help make negotiations go better later. "I explain that there's a right way and a wrong way to do this business," he says. "When customers come into the office, show them to the conference room and offer to get them a coffee or a soda. Be sure to turn to the receptionist and say, 'Please hold all my calls until we're done.'"

Bigelow says he urges new sales associates to say those words, even if they have no reason to believe anyone will be calling them. The point is to make sure the clients perceive they are the only ones you want to talk to for the next half hour. For the duration of the meeting, you need to make the sales presentation you (I hope) have practiced. Because new sales associates don't have any personal accomplishments to brag about, they need to rely heavily on the services offered by the company. Potential clients should be shown the company's Web site and, if you have one, your own Web site. Bigelow warns, however, that it is more important for the agent to listen than to talk.

Reading Buyers

"You need to say to a buyer, 'Tell me what you want, tell me how much you are willing to spend. Tell me about your likes and dislikes. And also tell me what Utopia would be. Tell me what would be perfect. I don't know if that house is out there, but if it is and we have an opportunity to buy it, I need to know what it is.'" Throughout the conversation, Bigelow advises the sales associate to take notes because they'll come in handy later. "As you are going through homes, you'll want to remind the buyer, 'this is the kind of view you said you'd like,' or 'this is the kind of kitchen you said you preferred.'" Also as part of that meeting, Bigelow recommends walking the buyer over to the company's mortgage officer, if it has one. In a matter of a few minutes, the mortgage broker can get a pretty good fix on how much home a buyer can afford.

Next, he says, set up a time to look for houses—preferably a time that is a few days away so you can set up a multihome tour that leads you back to your office at the end of the day. "At the beginning of the tour, you hand them a scorecard and ask them to rate all the homes they see on a 1-to-10 basis, with 1 being the dogs and 10 being perfect. At the end of the day, you want to sit down with them and discuss their scorecards. The first thing you're going to do is dump all the 1 through 5s. You want to concentrate on the 7s, 8s, and 9s—and 10s, if they have any."

Bigelow maintains that the reasons people give for not buying a house that otherwise suits them fall into three categories: a stall, an objection, and a condition.

1. **Stall:** "A stall is what they tell you if they don't want to tell you the real reason they don't want to buy. They'll say, 'I want to think about it a little longer,' or 'There may be

another home that is coming on the market.'"

2. **Objection:** "An objection is a real reason, but one that you can overcome. They'll say, 'I don't like the carpeting.' You can change the carpet. 'I don't like the color of the appliances.' You can get new ones. Or, I don't like the wallpaper,' or 'I don't like the dark paneling.' These are all things you can work with."

3. **Condition:** "A condition is an objection that you can't overcome. 'I like the house, but it's built on a busy street.' 'I like the house, but it's next to a commercial property.' 'I like the house, but it has two floors and my knees are bad.' You can't overcome conditions." Says Bigelow, "I teach people that 95 percent of all objections and conditions can be eliminated if you have a thorough discussion in your initial meeting. A doctor doesn't start operating on you before he finds out what's wrong. Real estate is the same thing. You need to know what your clients want."

There is a cliché in the industry, "buyers are liars," meaning that many buyers will tell you quite specifically what kind of house they need—and then buy something that doesn't bear the slightest resemblance to what they said they wanted. Bigelow, however, is philosophical.

"Everyone has the right to change their requirements. It happens more often than not. You've heard it before, but it's true. What sells houses is 'location, location, location.'"

Buyers may express a preference for older homes in established neighborhoods, but shun them when they see how little they get for so much money. Not unusually, a larger home in a less expensive neighborhood turns out to be much better. Location, location, location. By far the biggest frustration, says Bigelow, is that consumers simply don't know how the industry works—and other real estate professionals understand that only too well.

Wandering Buyers and the Wolf in Agent's Clothing

You'll spend the day showing homes to clients and part company that night, with you urging them to consider everything they've seen so that you can talk about it when you call them tomorrow. Tomorrow, however, they don't answer the phone and you don't manage to get in touch with them until the day after. After spending a few minutes being coy, they will confess, "I think we bought one yesterday."

Invariably, the buyers had gone out on their own, seen a 'For Sale' sign on an interesting-looking house, and contacted the agent for a closer look. The conversation usually goes something like this, says Bigelow:

"Did you tell the other agent you were working with me?"

"Yes, we were going to call you, but the agent said he was expecting two more offers to come in. He said we better move fast."

What the agent had done was close the deal by implying the buyers could lose the house if they waited too long. And it worked.

Another time, Bigelow said, a relative had announced to him that she and her husband were moving to the community and needed a house. "I looked up several properties and sent them to her. I told her to go ahead and drive by them and let me know if any of them looked interesting." She and her husband did drive by several, including one that looked very good. They noticed, however, that the sales office representing the house was just down the street, so they decided to stop in. On grilling, she conceded, they did not mention initially that they were working with another agent, and the broker they were talking to didn't ask.

After the broker showed them the property and they returned to the office to draw up the contract, the relative suddenly remembered she was working with another agent and the couple wanted to submit the contract through him.

The broker asked, "Did he show you the property?" The relative answered, "No," and the broker continued to write up the contract. Later the excited relative called Bigelow to announce she and her husband had purchased a house. The stunned Bigelow asked why she didn't wait for him, and was told, "Don't worry, the broker said he knew you and would be happy to let you look at it on our behalf later." Read that: *No commission.*

Another thing that sometimes happens is that homebuyers will see one of your listings while their agent is out of town. "Get to know [the customers]," Bigelow suggested. "Find out if they are working with the other agent as clients [under contract to him] or customers [not under contract]. They may say to you that they couldn't possibly submit an offer until their agent gets back into town. If they say that, it is OK for you to tell them that your office sells two houses per day and there is no guarantee that the house they like will still be there when the agent returns."

Often, said Bigelow, if you offer to pay the missing agent a referral fee, the buyers will go ahead with the deal.

"A lot of consumers just don't hear the soft sell," Bigelow said. "I will explain to my buyers, 'Now, I'm going to show you a lot of houses and I'm going to send you a lot of information. Some of the houses will be listed by my company, and some of them will be listed by other companies. I know you want to work through me and buy a house through me, but I also know you are going to want to go out and look at other homes on your own. If you go into another home when I'm not with you, tell the broker that you are working exclusively with me.'" Instead of doing that, he said, clients often will call their agent after they've seen another house and submitted a contract. "It's very difficult to undo that scenario," he said. "It raises a lot of issues about whether you should get paid a commission." Some agents also resort to tricks on the listing side to get the consumer's business.

Bigelow said if he knows in advance whom a seller is interviewing while deciding whom to list with, it often helps him put together a competitive presentation.

"You get to know the other brokers in town and how they work," Bigelow said. "I know that if I'm giving a listing presentation and other offices may also be giving presentations, I'm going to know that the office down the street is good and professional, that our presentations will be similar, our comparative market analyses will be in the same ballpark so we'll probably both suggest about the same asking price. But I also might know that the other company making a presentation is known to cut commissions.

"If I know that, I'm going to find a way to mention in my presentation that part of the commission is used to market the property. I don't mention any names, but I tell them that if some other company says they can sell the house for less, it usually means they are going to have to cut corners somewhere. They aren't going to advertise the house completely. They may not do a complete marketing job. I tell them that we do a complete marketing job and because of it, the seller can expect more competition and a higher price."

The idea, says Bigelow, is to undermine the commission-cutting broker before he ever starts his presentation.

Procuring Cause

There are two words that are going to guide much of your career. They are the words *procuring cause*. Your income depends on those words. "Procuring cause" literally asks the question, "Who was the procuring cause of the sale?" And, by implication, "Who is entitled to a portion of the commission?"

If you introduced the house to the buyer, helped negotiate the deal, and guided it to closing, there usually is no question that you are the procuring cause of the sale and you are entitled to a share of the commission.

Things get more vague, however, if the buyers are out looking on their own, see a house they like, and fail to call you to help negotiate the deal. The cliché in the industry used to be "nobody owns a buyer," which essentially meant that if you weren't with the buyer when the deal happened, you weren't entitled to get paid.

With the advent of buyer brokerage, however, procuring cause has become more complicated. Many buyer agents are now having their buyers sign legal contracts tying them together in the transaction. The contracts literally are an agreement between the agent and the buyer that the agent will get paid for his services, no matter what home is purchased and no matter how involved the buyer agent is in the deal. Buyer agents say the contracts are needed to keep listing agents from manipulating buyers as they look at homes. Listing agents, however, ask why buyer agents should get paid if they neither show the house nor write up the purchase offer.

Chapter 12

How Come Nobody Likes Me?

Time to polish the image

There's good news, bad news, and good news. The good news is that you're either getting or have gotten your real estate license. With some decent training, some hard work, and a little luck, you can quite legitimately make a lot of money in this business.

The bad news is—oh, let's just face it—you're a real estate agent. And if you haven't learned it already, that means almost nobody outside the industry is going to respect you (and not many inside the industry, either). It means that your job is the butt of jokes on late-night TV and movies everywhere.

But the final good news is that now that you're here, you can help change that.

Let's just attack this head-on. If you look across the broad spectrum of American culture, few professions are held in lower esteem than the one you've chosen. In the entertainment media, real estate people are characterized as hustlers and buffoons, occasionally as lovable but bumbling con men, bad dressers with bad hairdos, not very bright, not very hard-working, and always out to make a buck— no matter whose body they have to step over to make it.

Needless to say, that's not you—nor is it 99 percent of the people you work with.

That lack of respect, however, is reinforced on an almost annual basis by the Gallup polling organization, which every January releases its report on America's most revered professions. Real estate agents are not near the top or even in the middle. They aren't last, but they are inevitably in the bottom third. You can expect to be listed somewhere ahead of used-car salesmen, and close to lawyers and congressmen. When your friends are shaking their heads and your grandmother is lamenting that you could have been somebody, it's hard to keep in mind that stereotypes are just that—attempts to lump people into comfortable cubbyholes.

Not all real estate agents are ruthless, just as not all doctors are smart and not all bankers are honest. Likewise, not all lawyers are crooks, not all hair dressers are gay and some accountants actually have very interesting lives.

As you'll see as you gain time in the business, the response to the image problem inside the industry has been predictably split— and odds are you will find yourself falling into one of two camps: Either you'll be among those who will work to change the image of the industry or you'll shrug it off with a simple, "Why bother?" Says Debbie Long, "There are a lot of agents who just decide to laugh all the way to the bank. They figure the image is wrong. It's not them. But there's nothing they can do about it."

D e b b i e   L o n g ■
Ethics and Stereotypes

Long is one of the nation's best-known teachers of real estate ethics, and her core belief is that such disrespect does hurt the industry and that, over time, efforts to improve the industry's reputation can be beneficial.

Three of Debbie's reasons why brokers and agents need to improve their images:

1. "The public is demanding higher ethical conduct from business professionals. Contemporary headlines indicate that the public is outraged by recent business scandals and the notorious conduct of businesspeople."

2. "Legislatures continue to coerce practitioners to virtue by enacting oppressive legislation. When a profession does not guard its own reputation and acts in such a way as to harm the public, state legislatures respond by creating new state laws. For example, because real estate agents failed to be completely honest with purchasers regarding their agency relationships, state legislatures enacted agency disclosure laws that required massive paperwork and documentation."

3. "The number of complaints against individual licensees registered with their state licensing boards is increasing. Many of the problems created by licensees have an ethical—as well as a legal—dimension."

Long has spent years researching how agents got such dismal reputations. Invariably, she says, it starts with education, or a lack thereof. "The bar to entry into real estate is very low. The time it takes to get a license is linked directly to public perception that real estate agents are poorly educated," she believes.

In most states it takes 45 to 60 hours of prelicense school work to get a license, and most states require only a handful of additional courses every few years to keep your license intact. Compare that with the years it takes to become a lawyer or doctor, or even an accountant, and you'll begin to see why people tend to look down their noses at real estate agents.

A second issue, says Long, is compensation. "The public thinks we earn more than we do. They don't understand how we are paid. A seller sees the agent take a check for $14,000 but doesn't understand that the agent is going to get 25 percent of that—before taxes and expenses." Long also is a critic of those "Million Dollar Club" advertisements that she says continue to send the wrong message to the public. "I've heard of those things winding up in divorce court. Some judge thinks an agent is making a million dollars a year. That's the perception those ads send." Long also considers the ads "tacky and sleazy." "Can you imagine an oncologist advertising he did $100 million in cancer treatments last year?"

Third, Long blames the media for reinforcing the stereotypical real estate agent image in such movies as *American Beauty, The Money Pit* and others where agents are depicted as being unsympathetic and often unsavory characters. That's why, she says, every year the National Association of REALTORS® spends millions of dollars in a national advertising campaign trying to counteract the negative portrayals of agents. The REALTORS® attempt to show that most agents actually are hard-working and needed consultants in what for most people is a very difficult transitional period—the move from one home to another.

Long is seeking more education for incoming agents, as well as continuing education after they're in the business, and notes that there are studies suggesting that the better-educated a license holder is, the higher regard they have for ethics in the business—translating into a better public image. As a direct result of those studies and a task force formed to look into the image of real estate agents, NAR began requiring its members to take 2.5 hours of Code of Ethics training every four years to maintain their REALTOR® membership. That, says Long, is better than nothing.

But Long also points to a more interesting study by the Georgia Real Estate Commission in 1997 that suggests that maybe more education is not the only answer to what ails the real estate industry image. Maybe it also has a lot to do with how real estate people—including you—run their businesses.

Charles Clark ■

Doing the Right Thing

A **few years** ago Georgia Real Estate Commissioner Charles Clark discussed the agency's findings with a group of real estate educators, who were fascinated by the results.

Every year, the Georgia commission staff conducts between 1,500 and 2,000 investigations, mostly on the basis of complaints filed by the public. Year after year, Clark said, approximately 50 percent of the investigations actually turned up no violation of the law. The staff also concluded that about 40 percent of the investigations discovered only minor technical violations of the law that resulted in no harm to the public and required only warning letters from the commission to the licensee.

Only 10 percent of the investigations resulted in formal disciplinary actions.

In trying to reason out why the numbers came up as they did, Clark concluded, first, that some people always feel they are being victimized in business dealings. "Thus, rather than trying to figure out how they can resolve the problem directly with another party, they immediately call in the state regulators," he said.

Second, he theorized, because the majority of complaints actually turned out to involve no violation of law, the study suggested that even the most minimally competent agents were at least smart enough to stay within the bounds of legality as they tried to do business.

Third, Clark believed the numbers indicated that most license holders were, in fact, moral and ethical and would do the "right thing" if they knew what the right thing was. That, he felt, was clearly a suggestion that more education could help agents know the right thing to do. What the commission did then, however, was truly inspired. Although it had established that most complaints did not involve violations of the law, the commission took a next step—to figure out what was triggering the complaints in the first place.

What it found was, to put it bluntly, lousy service on the part of license holders.

"For example," he told the educators, "an investigation [of a complaint] revealed that a broker did not return an earnest money payment for two months after she received a written demand . . . There were some extenuating circumstances that explained, if not justified, the delay. Buried in the investigation was a statement from the buyer that he was not concerned as much about the delay as that no one had explained to him the reason for the delay."

As Clark and his staff dug into the complaints, a curious pattern evolved—one that had little to do with the law. The complaints were filled with remarks such as the following:

- He wouldn't return my telephone calls.
- She didn't address us as Mr. and Mrs.
- He stopped by our house unannounced.
- I don't know why she waited two days to present our offer.
- He showed up in a running suit.
- She talked down to me.
- He was late for every appointment.
- She turned me over to someone else for everything.
- He didn't explain what that meant.
- She was rude about everything.
- He wasted our time showing houses that we had no interest in.
- We never could reach her.
- He never seemed to care about the problem.

If these were the things that were triggering complaints, Clark concluded, more education for real estate agents on state laws would not reduce the number of complaints coming to the commission. It appeared that what was really needed was a class in business manners and etiquette.

Larry Romito ■

Toward a Solution

It will come as no surprise that many in the industry already are working at trying to fix the image that real estate professionals project. Better-educated licensees is one approach; the REALTOR® association's mass-media campaign is another.

Yet another effort is being made by ultimate industry insider Larry Romito in San Juan Capistrano, California. Romito has served as president of the national Council of Residential Brokers, and he built his early career as one of those who turned the Coldwell Banker name into an international powerhouse.

To the consternation of industry leaders who prefer the status quo, Romito believes the only thing wrong with the real estate industry today is that it's built upside down: It honors the salesman and discards the consumer.

Says Romito, "All of the industry's awards, rewards, and compensation are directed at the people with the most production, doing the most deals, and closing the most transactions. What we talk about is 'top producers,' but the way we define that is by x number of sales, x number of transactions, and x amount of commission generated. That's one of the problems. Nobody ever talks about the quality of those deals. They talk about whether the top producer was satisfied—yeah, he was satisfied, he made money—but no one ever talks about whether his consumers were satisfied. Did they find the experience rewarding? Nobody ever really asks whether the consumer was happy."

Romito maintains that real estate agents are missing opportunities to construct long-term business relationships by disappearing from the customer's life as soon as the transaction is over. He notes that agents and families often work days together to find a suitable home. They eat lunch together, get to know each other's children, and go through intense negotiating sessions together, but in the end the agent disappears as soon as the commission check clears. Not much of a friendship. The consumer may feel jilted, but the industry is hardly in a position to do anything about it.

"You have to have standards, accountability, and deadlines in any industry. Otherwise, you end up in chaos. But in real estate, when a broker says to an agent, 'You have to accept my standards,' the independent contractor says, 'No, I don't.' What happens then is that the broker has to decide whether he wants the independent contractor's production, or whether he wants to enforce standards. Usually the decision is to keep the production."

The downside, says Romito, is that real estate has become an industry that provides service by biorhythm. "If the agent feels like working today, great. If he doesn't, too bad. Maybe he feels like showing a listing, maybe he doesn't. And nobody is going to require him to." The result, he says, is that consumers have come to learn that in real estate—arguably the biggest money transaction they'll ever commit to—they cannot depend on getting even the basics of what they can get from any fast-food restaurant: "Consistent, reliable, predictable, accountable, and responsive service." No wonder the industry has a bad reputation. Romito's solution has been the creation of a "Qualify Service Certification" program that surveys consumers on the performance of member real estate agents and posts their ratings to a public Web site: www.qualityservice.org.

To be a part of the system, however, you have to agree to jump through some hoops that the industry has not had to jump through before—hoops that Romito defends as being fundamental to every other successful business in the world.

Making Promises, Making the Grade

Explains Romito, "You have to tell the consumer in writing what you're going to do. And you have to guarantee it in writing. And you have to do that with every transaction you're involved in, not just this one or that one. Your goal is to provide consistent, reliable, predictable service to every consumer."

The program requires that you tell consumers what you are going to do, and back up your promises in writing.

- Explain how you are going to legally represent them in the transaction.
- Provide a written, detailed comparative market analysis.
- Help sellers make an intelligent decision on pricing.
- Help sellers prepare a written, accurate property condition report.
- Provide written suggestions on ways to enhance curb appeal.
- Provide a written marketing plan on what you are going to do to get the property sold.
- Explain the frequency of communication with consumers and how that communication will take place.
- Help them negotiate price and terms.
- Promise to pay attention to detail: the escrow accounting, title, closing, and so forth.
- Attend the closing if legally permitted.
- Guarantee the service.
- Advise consumers that they will be asked to evaluate the service they receive at the end of the transaction.

Two important things happen, Romito says. "If I know I'm going to be graded, I'm going to do a better job. Second, if the consumer knows he's going to be grading me, he's paying more attention to what I'm doing. He's checking off the services I've provided." As part of the program, which costs agents $250 to participate in, an independent research company conducts a survey, asking the consumer to rate the services received on a 1 to 5 level. Agents who cannot maintain above a 3.75 level of satisfaction are asked to leave the program. "Consumers go into every transaction expecting to be satisfied," Romito says. "So just having a satisfied customer can't be the goal. You have to have a *very* satisfied customer."

And that, he says, will lead to more repeat business and referrals—and also a better image for the real estate business.

The Organized You

It's true: Give and you shall receive

I f you let it, the real estate business will make you a better
person.

No, that doesn't sound quite right.

If you become a better person, you will have your real estate
career to thank for it.

No, that doesn't sound quite right, either. One more try.

For you to flourish as an individual, you need to have a genuine interest in your community—and if you take a genuine
interest in your community, you may well find that your real
estate career will flourish, as well.

Yes, that's much closer.

A new real estate agent spends a lot of time looking down. You
look down at forms, trying to figure them out. You look down at
listing sheets and advertising flyers. But while all those things are
terribly important to your career, try to remember that—even
from the very beginning—your business isn't in the office, it's out
in your community. The people who are going to buy or sell
houses through you are out there somewhere. It's unlikely that a
single one of them is actually hanging around your office. The
best way to find them is to be out there among them. Looking
down is important, but sometimes you have to look *out*.

Put better by top producer Judy Blevins, "A real estate agent—even a new real estate agent—is better off slapping on a name tag and going out and buying her groceries than she is just sitting in the office making calls. Networking is what works in this business. You need to talk about what you do for a living. Let people know you're in real estate."

Judy Blevins ■

Getting Involved

Arguably one of the best ways to network in your community is to become a part of it, and one of the best ways to become a part of it, says Blevins, is to join an organization that is doing something to help its fellow citizens. Have faith; whatever you give will come back to you in ways you never expect.

Blevins, a sales associate for Coldwell Banker Residential Brokerage in Aberdeen, Maryland, knows that it's true. She has networked her way to being one of the most successful agents in the ERA franchise system. She credits her success to her involvement in her community. In response to her good works, her community nominated her for national recognition among REALTOR® members.

For the 16 years she has been in the business, Blevins has worked among the community's poor—trying to find, and create if necessary, decent housing for all—even if it means banging on the federal government's door with grant proposals. She unabashedly credits her work among her neighbors as a reason her career has soared. "I'm very involved with the renovation of homes for resale in parts of the community that are considered less than desirable," she says. "I work closely with town administrators and the chamber of commerce. I write grant proposals trying to get money from the government. We try to get more police so communities feel safer. If communities are safer, neighborhoods become more desirable and pretty soon people want to live there."

If you ask Blevins a "chicken or the egg" question about which came first, social consciousness or business acumen, she shrugs. "It actually feels very strange," she says. "I get nominated for all my community work, but I'm sitting here thinking, 'Wait a minute, but I'm making money here. This is what I do for a living.'"

Like so many other real estate agents when they are first starting out, Blevins had no natural niche she could exploit to develop her business. She realized, however, that she needed to make contacts, so one of the first things she did was join the local Chamber of Commerce. As a member of the Chamber, it seemed reasonable that she would become involved in the housing committee, where she already had an interest, and that in turn put her in touch with community leaders who also were interested in the community's housing problems. Almost without realizing it, her network began to form. Charitable contacts started turning into social contacts, and before long social contacts began turning into business contacts.

Best of all, she says, she was doing something she believed in. All she did was take action on an interest she already had, which happened to be an interest in an area where the community needed help. "I started going to meetings and getting involved. Pretty soon you find that you start getting into [whatever cause needs you] and you forget that one of the reasons you started was that you wanted to meet people." The more meetings she had to attend, the more the issue became a personal crusade. The more people who heard her passion about the issue, the stronger her reputation became, which led to more business contacts. In fact, her reputation was so solid that a housing developer who renovated some 300 rental homes and put them on the market for sale considered no one but her to represent the project. Blevins acknowledges that real estate is a business you have to have a personality for. "It's hard in the beginning. You have to push yourself to get out there," she says. "You have to make yourself visible and be out there in the community. But you also have to let people know you're in business and you have a product to sell and that product is yourself.

"It's important to be honest with people. That's the biggest downfall I see among new agents. They just aren't honest with you, and people can tell and they don't want to do business with you." As a single mother with two children who were small when she was trying to start her career, she sympathizes with others who are forced to make difficult family decisions.

"They both suffered because I wasn't around sometimes. In the beginning, I was working six days per week. But you have to do it when you're starting out. You need to put the time in. You need to have a business plan. You need to decide what you want out of your career and then figure out how to get it. For me to get where I wanted to be, I had to get involved in my community."

Trisha Millett Fletcher ■

The Importance of Being Real

Trisha Millett Fletcher of Coldwell Banker Millett in Auburn, Maine, also believes community involvement and real estate success are close to the same thing. And she agrees wholeheartedly that it's important for new agents to be out in their communities even more than being in the office.

"When you're first starting out is the time you really need to be out in the community, becoming involved in the Chamber of Commerce, doing volunteer work at the hospital, being involved in organizations that interest you," she says. What kick-started her career was her involvement in local charity work. She volunteered at the hospital and met a large number of people that way. She became involved in the chamber of commerce and served on a number of committees. Fletcher also took up golf for the purpose of meeting people and became involved in a women's golf league. "It's important for people to know you're a real estate agent, but it's also important for people to see you in a different light—as a volunteer or a golf partner." Volunteer work and personal marketing often go hand in hand. Many real estate agents volunteer to be ushers at community theaters or take tickets at charitable events.

But they also usually wear name tags that identify them as real estate agents—not just their companies, but themselves.

"It's important to establish your name, your logo, and your face in your community," says Fletcher. "Even if people aren't in the market for a house right now, they will start remembering you. People will come up to you and say, 'I see your name everywhere. You must be doing a lot of business.' That's what you want to have happen. It's part of building your image."

Fletcher also emphasizes, however, that if you do become involved in community work, don't try to fake it. It is important to be part of something you believe in or that you have a connection to. People can tell if you lack sincerity or belong to a group only because you plan to mine it for commission fees.

The National Association of REALTORS®

As an important caveat, and one with very serious business overtones, Fletcher believes strongly in becoming involved in the National Association of REALTORS®, the trade association that most active real estate agents join. In fact, the NAR is the largest trade association in the country.

Fletcher's mother, Sharon Millett, is a former president of the organization, and Fletcher also has become involved. Regardless of whether you, as a new agent, ever decide to pursue a role in the governance of the group, you should at the very least join the NAR and become as active as you can on a volunteer basis. (Most real estate brokerages are members of the NAR, and you quite likely will have an opportunity to become a member within the first few days after you begin work. It will cost you a couple of hundred dollars, but it's well worth it.)

"I found that being involved at the state REALTOR® level was very beneficial, even as a new agent," Fletcher says. "I started working on REALTOR® committees with other real estate agents from around the state. As you get to know other professionals, they start getting to know you and trusting your judgment. Pretty soon you have REALTORS® whom you've done volunteer work with who are sending you referrals. There is a direct business link with a REALTOR® membership. It's very important to be involved."

Chapter 14

Business Cards and Alphabet Soup

It's not the letters that are important, it's the numbers they represent

Just as an interesting exercise, collect as many business cards as you possibly can. Get your broker's card and the cards of the people around you. When you go out on broker tours, get cards from everybody in the car. But instead of just shoving them into your pocket, take a moment to really look at the card—making special note of the initials that follow the names. Those letters represent certifications and designations the card owners have received over the years, usually related to some specialty they've developed or some education they've participated in. These letters are, essentially, advanced degrees in real estate.

When you are first starting out, advanced designations may not seem very important to you. After all, you just got out of real estate school, and you're in no hurry to go back for more. Plus, quite frankly, additional designations and certifications can be expensive. There is a cost to the coursework involved. You usually have to travel to another city to take the course. There will be money spent on lodging if it is a two-or-more-day course.

Nevertheless, the longer you are in the business, the more you are going to find that some of these initials are really worth having—and the sooner the better. Not to be at all subtle about it: Some of these designations are worth money to you—sometimes a

lot of money, and often in ways you don't even think about.
First, a couple of quick definitions.

- A **certification** is something that has to do with a specific set of skills that you learn, skills that are usable across a variety of different real estate specialties.
- A **designation,** on the other hand, usually involves specific training for a specific discipline. For instance, you can be accredited as a buyer representative or as a financial or residential specialist.

Now that you know the difference, you might as well know something else as well: There are no certification or designation rules. In your career, you will be involved in many classes that seem like certification courses for which you will actually receive designations; and you'll take many designation courses that have the look and feel of a certification. There are no Certification/ Designation Police.

What also is worth knowing is this: According to a National Association of REALTORS® survey, sales agents holding professional designations have annual incomes that are, on average, $18,100 higher than those of sales associates who do not have designations. Certifications and designations do you a lot of good, and not just because of the education in the classroom.

As RE/MAX International President Daryl Jesperson (ABR, CRB, CRP) explains, designations are one of the things that set you apart from the sales associates you are competing against.

D a r y l   J e s p e r s o n ■

Finding Credibility

"**L**et's be honest, what new sales associates lack is credibility. In the beginning, when you're out there marketing yourself, you can say you work for the best broker in town, or the biggest broker, or you know the neighborhood the best, or you have the quirkiest phone number, but you don't really have anything of

substance that separates you from everybody else. But a professional designation does that. It shows that you have spent some
extra time and money and energy to gain some additional knowledge about your business. That's something real that you can
explain to consumers.

"A second very big thing about designations is that they give
you a chance to expand your personal network—not just beyond
your own company, but even beyond your own city. That leads to
more income." Most of the time, courses that result in certifications or designations are sponsored by local or state REALTOR®
associations. They are an excellent opportunity to talk with
agents from other companies and other parts of the state.
Contacts such as these often lead to referral business.

The large franchises also offer the same courses specifically
for their members, as do the larger of the independent real
estate companies. What you'll find is that people who receive
designations often form affinity groups that are as strong as
their company or franchise ties. It is not unusual for a Century 21
Certified Residential Specialist (CRS) in New York to refer business to a CRS in Chicago who may work for an independent
company. Why?

"Because they both understand the quality of training they
had to go through to get the CRS," explains Jesperson. "They
usually know when they pass on the referral—even if they don't
personally know the person they are sending it to, which they
often do—that the CRS on the receiving end has been trained to
work with clients in the way they want them to be worked with."
(Some holders of the CRS swear it is best to take the course work
for this particular designation "out of town." If you take the class
in your own community, they say, you will be sitting with people
you compete with. If you take the classes in other cities, however,
it gives you a chance to network with those people and dramati-
cally improves your chances of getting referrals.)

In saying that, however, it needs to be noted that not all designations are created equal. Because the National Association of
REALTORS® is so large, designations and certifications that it rec-
ognizes tend to carry more weight, and they are certainly more
recognizable among fellow REALTORS®. They are advertised more

and appear on Web sites more often. There are, however, many fine programs offered by other organizations and even private companies that are worth investigating.

R o n n   H u t h ■

Being Realistic about Designations

"The courses are expensive. And some of them take years to get," Jesperson said. "But a lot of times, one referral will more than pay for all your expenses."

What you won't get from a real estate designation, however, is much public recognition. Real estate broker Ronn Huth (ABR, ABRM, CRS, GRI, ePRO, CEBA, MCBA, CBB, CBR), of South Hamilton, Massachusetts, who has earned many designations over his 15 years in the business, cautions that it's unlikely that such things as the General Accredited Appraiser (GAA) will ever become household names.

"The reason you should get a designation is for the education, not for the money," he says. "Especially if you are in a smaller firm that does not offer a lot of training, what you can learn in some of these courses can make a huge difference in your career and your ability to serve the public."

Huth recommends that every new REALTOR® member sign up for the GRI–the Graduate, REALTOR® Institute designation that is available in every state. "This is the basic designation. This is the one that gets you started. It gives you the basics of the real estate business. New agents should be encouraged to take this right away."

Because Huth's company, Buyers Choice Realty, works extensively with homebuyers, he urges his agents to take the Accredited Buyer Representative (ABR) course soon after earning their GRI. "I want them to take the ABR because I don't want them stumbling into some liability issues," he says candidly. There are more extensive buyer agent courses, such as those offered by the National Association of Exclusive Buyer Agents, but Huth recommends the ABR first to his agents to get the basics.

He also has a high degree of confidence in the CRS course offered by the Council of Residential Specialists—an NAR affiliated group. The CRS, however, is harder to get than most designations—only about 5 percent of the 800,000 members of the REALTOR® association have the designation. While it might be OK to list a few designations on your business card—ones you will want to include in your listing presentations or presentations to buyers— "You can overdo it," says Huth. "If you put too many on there, people will get overwhelmed. What people want to know is that you've taken the time to educate yourself in your specialty. That means you've done something that is going to help them either buy a house or sell one. Beyond that, it gets pretty confusing."

Following is a brief sampling of certifications and designations currently available to real estate professionals. There are many others as well, and new ones are emerging every day. Remember: Some programs require extensive and costly class hours. In some cases, it can take years to complete designation course requirements, and once you have a designation, most of them must be renewed either every year or every two years. There may be books to buy and exams to take at the end of the course. Some also require that you complete a certain number of transactions before you qualify. Also, there is no guarantee that all classes will be offered in a city near you, so you may have to travel. More and more courses are being offered via the Internet. Be sure to check with the vendor.

Designations and certifications in the following list that are recognized by the National Association of REALTORS® are marked with a +. (Please note, though, that just because a particular designation is included in this list, or is not included, doesn't mean that this book's author or publisher is making any judgment regarding their value or effectiveness.)

ABR +

Accredited Buyer Representative, offered by the Real Estate Buyer's Agent Council, *www.rebac.net*

ABRM +

Accredited Buyer Representative Manager, offered by REBAC, *www.rebac.net*

AHWD +

At Home with Diversity Certification, offered by the National Association of REALTORS® and the Department of Housing and UrbanDevelopment, *http://nar.realtor.com/community/diversity*

ALC +

Accredited Land Consultant, offered by the REALTORS® Land Institute, *www.rliland.com*

CCIM +

Certified Commercial Investment Member, offered by the Commercial Investment Real Estate Institute (CIREI), *www.ccim.com*

C-CREC

Certified Consumer Real Estate Consultant, offered by the National Association of Real Estate Consultants, *www.narec.org*

CEBA

Certified Exclusive Buyer Agent, offered by the National Association of Exclusive Buyer Agents, *www.naeba.org*

CIPS +

Certified International Property Specialist, offered by the National Association of REALTORS®, *www.cipsnetwork.com*

CPM +

Certified Property Manager, offered by the Institute of Real Estate Management, *www.irem.org*

CRB +

Certified Real Estate Brokerage Manager, offered by the Real Estate Brokerage Managers Council, *www.crb.com*

CRE+

Counselor of Real Estate, offered by the Counselors of Real Estate, *ww.cre.org*

CREA

Certified Real Estate Appraiser, offered by the National Association of Real Estate Appraisers, *http://iami.org/narea.html*

CRP

Certified Relocation Professional, offered by the Employee Relocation Council, *www.erc.org*

CRS +

Certified Residential Specialist, offered by the Council of Residential Specialists, *www.crs.com*

DREI

Distinguished Real Estate Instructor, offered by the Real Estate Educators Association, *www.reea.org*

e-PRO+

e-PRO, offered by the Internet Crusade, *www.internetcrusade.com*

GAA +

General Accredited Appraiser, offered by the National Association of REALTORS®, *www.narappraisalsource.com*

GRI +

Graduate, REALTOR® Institute, offered by state REALTOR® associations; see state REALTOR® association Web sites

LTG +

Leadership Training Graduate, offered by the Women's Council of REALTORS®, *www.wcr.org*

QSC

Quality Service Certified, offered by Quality Service Certification Inc., *www.qualityservice.org*

RAA+

Residential Accredited Appraiser, offered by the National Association of REALTORS®, *www.narappraisalsource.com*

RCE +

REALTOR® association Certified Executive, offered by the National Association of REALTORS®, *RCEonline.com*

SIOR +

Society of Industrial and Office REALTORS®, offered by the Society of Industrial and Office REALTORS®, *www.sior.com*

SRES

Seniors Real Estate Specialists, Senior Advantage Real Estate Council, *www.seniorsrealestate.com*

Chapter 15

Like Scorpions Circling in a Bottle

Lawyers: Can't live with 'em, can't live without 'em

Two of the more interesting relationships you'll develop during your career are the ones between you and the lawyers representing your clients and the ones between you and the home inspectors who comb through houses looking for problems. Eventually, the phrase "deal killers" will spring to your lips.

Lawyers and inspectors are living proof of the universal law that "every action has an equal and opposite reaction." Put into real estate jargon: For every real estate agent who sees a great deal coming together quickly and easily, there is a lawyer or a home inspector ready to step in and say, "Not so fast."

Are they really deal killers? They can be. On the other hand, as you'll learn as you go through your professional life, some deals—even some attractive deals—really need to be killed. Roughly 80 percent of all lawsuits brought against real estate agents start as disputes over property defects. Clearly there was a breakdown somewhere.

Property Disclosure

From the real estate agent's perspective, whether you are working with the buyer or the seller, there really are two very good things happening in the industry. First, in more and more states, home sellers are being required to fill out property defect disclosure forms. And second, a steadily increasing number of purchase agreements are coming in with inspection contingency clauses.

No matter which side of the transaction you are on, you need to have a positive attitude about disclosures and inspectors, even though sellers historically don't like either. Disclosure forms and home inspections help protect you, the agent, from legal liability.

The forms provided by states are simple and straightforward: Does the roof leak? Does the basement flood? Some innovative real estate companies are going beyond those state requirements, developing their own forms. The forms may go into drainage issues and questions about appliances. They may ask how old the roof is and not only whether it leaks now but whether it ever did.

The reason sellers hate the forms is that every defect revealed, every little "eccentricity" of the house, can translate into a reduction in the price of the home. Nevertheless, you should urge your seller to fill out the form as honestly and completely as possible. The seller needs to confess that the basement floods or that the roof leaks or that when he personally rewired the den, all the switches were put in backward and, no, there was never any professional inspection of his work. As an agent, you need to keep in mind that every defect that is not disclosed is a potential lawsuit—not only against the seller but also against you.

Which brings us to home inspections.

Because homesellers are not always candid on their property disclosure forms, buyers should get the home inspected by a professional, not by a friend or a relative.

Any agents representing buyers always should recommend that the buyers have a professional home inspection done. Buyer agents should make sure that such recommendations are put in writing and that the homebuyers sign a piece of paper stating that the agent urged them to have a home inspected before proceeding with the transaction.

Most homebuyers will not balk at having the home inspected. In fact, when you suggest it, usually the very next thing that will happen is that they'll ask you to recommend an inspector. Here it is important to follow the lead of your supervising broker. Some companies do not want their agents to get involved with making recommendations of home inspectors. Those companies believe that if you recommend an inspector, and the inspector misses something in his or her inspection, you—the agent—and the company could be held liable. When buyers ask for a recommendation, some companies believe you should just hand them the phone book and tell them to pick one. Other companies will provide a buyer with a list of six or seven inspectors and suggest that the buyer make a choice from those.

The Home Inspection

Who should attend the home inspection? Absolutely everybody should be invited. In addition to the inspector, the inspection should include the homebuyer, the buyer agent, and the listing agent. Even the sellers should be welcomed, though the listing agent will probably discourage the seller from being present and the inspector may not want all those people supervising—but you don't always get what you want in life.

As a practical matter, even if all those people gather at the beginning of the inspection, most of them eventually are going to drift off. Home inspections actually are kind of boring if you're not the inspector and you're not the buyer.

You may find that you are perfectly happy to wait outside by your car as the inspector and buyer crawl around the house. Feel free to use your cell phone to talk with other clients and make other appointments. However, you probably are going to want to be physically present at the inspection. The reason is that it's often at the inspection that the deal comes unglued. You need to be there to patch it up.

If you are the listing agent in the deal, you probably are going to be more nervous than the buyer agent. You weren't in a position to recommend a home inspector; you have no control over what the inspector will find; even worse, you're never really completely 100 percent confident that your sellers have told you the complete truth about their home, either verbally or on the signed disclosure forms. The "I forgots" seem to run rampant on the seller side of the deal.

Nevertheless, if you're new, you should probably try to participate as much as possible in the inspection, although the buyer may not want you there. A better use of your time is either keeping the sellers calm and out of the way or working your cell phone to find your next deal. The inspection is what it is. You'll get a copy of the report, and if you need to reopen negotiations, the buyer's agent will let you know.

B o b   B a s s   ■

Lawyers and Scorpions

Bob Bass, one of the nation's top real estate attorneys, likens the relationship between lawyers and agents to "two scorpions circling in a bottle." Even if they mean each other no harm, suspicion runs high, tension is extreme, and the word *trust* is almost never spoken.

However, from the National Association of REALTORS® on down to your own supervising broker, sales associates are urged to tell consumers (and feel free to memorize this line), "Remember, you have the right to have a lawyer review all the paperwork before you sign anything—and I highly recommend that you do so." While you're at it, memorize these words too, and speak them often: "If any legal questions come up at any point in the transaction, please feel free to contact your lawyer."

Working with a client's lawyer can be a real pain, even though you theoretically are on the same side. The most important thing to remember is that as long as there is a lawyer looking at everything, your legal exposure is reduced. But also remember, as long as there is a lawyer looking at everything, the deal could take a long time to close and may never close at all. It depends on the lawyer, and it depends on the deal. As a real estate agent, one of the most important phrases you will ever speak is this one: "I don't know."

If a legal question comes up about a contract, repeat the words, "I don't know." Do not try to bluff your way out of something, and never tell a client "The law is on your side." Almost always, the law is what the judge and the statute books say it is, not what the real estate agent says.

You do yourself a favor by recommending that your client be in frequent communication with a lawyer, but you do yourself and your client a disservice if you suggest they contact a lawyer who is not a real estate lawyer. You wouldn't go to an ophthalmologist for open heart surgery. You shouldn't send a client with a real estate problem to a divorce lawyer.

The ironic thing is that most consumers, no matter what they're told, will not, in fact, seek out legal counsel from a lawyer. Most people, says Bass, believe they are paying too much for a real estate agent already and don't want to be billed more for a lawyer.

Bass believes the idea that lawyers are "deal killers" is overblown, but concedes it is a lawyer's job to represent a client. "If a client calls her lawyer in his office and says, 'Hey, I'm in the middle of a real estate deal—can you get me out of it?' then the lawyer is going to do whatever he can to get his client out of it. On the other hand, if a lawyer gets a call and his client says, 'Hey, I'm in the middle of a real estate deal and there are some things I don't understand,' then is the lawyer going to try to kill that deal? Of course not."

Finally, Bass says, new agents should not panic if and when trouble comes their way.

The phone may ring, and it may be an angry former client. New agents will want to (1) help the former client to make sure the problem goes away because (2) they don't want their supervising broker to know they've fouled up.

According to Bass, those are both the wrong things to do.

The first thing you should do in such a situation is to find out where the caller can be reached so you may call back. Second, discuss the call with your supervising broker and tell the complete truth—no matter how embarrassing. Depending on company policy, your next call may be to the company attorney.

What you do *not* want to do is accept responsibility for something that may not be your fault. Nor should you commit your company to a course of action that it may not want to take. Says Bass, "When agents try to be helpful, that's when you get into trouble. If the client has a legal problem, then the client needs to see a lawyer. You [the sales agent] should not be lured into giving legal advice. And you should not recommend that your client call your lawyer, because if you get sued, you want your lawyer to represent you."

Like scorpions in a jar.

Chapter 16

Alien Life Forms

*Just because you're different doesn't mean
you don't fit in*

Unlike in the past, suddenly there seems to be no "wrong way" to do real estate. Options are everywhere. Yes, of course, there are rules, but philosophically the industry is opening up to fresh ideas and new methods of doing things. More than ever before, the real estate business is accommodating the way you want to work with consumers and, more important, the way consumers want to work with real estate professionals.

You can certainly keep doing it the traditional way. That means that when the deal is done, the total commission is divided somewhere around 50/50, with you getting half and the agent on the other side of the table getting half. You take your half and divide it again with your company according to some prearranged (but flexible) formula. The vast majority of real estate deals are still done that way. But now there are so many other ways to do business, as well. After you have some experience and some success, you may want to move to some kind of 100-percent-commission shop where you keep both your and your company's share of the commission in exchange for paying your company a "desk fee."

"Exclusive buyer brokerage" also seems to be gaining in popularity, with more agents switching to that kind of business all the time. On the horizon is a relatively new idea of compensation called *fee-for-service*, which is exactly what it sounds like. For every function you perform, such as preparing a comparative market analysis or chauffeuring a buyer around town, you charge your client a specific fee.

And, of course, the notion of paying real estate agents fixed salaries continues to be toyed with. In fact, many insiders look around the industry and say salaried agents is definitely the wave of the future.

As you continue to negotiate your career path, here are a few quick looks at some of the alternatives to traditional real estate.

100 Percent Commission

Almost without exception, the 100-percent-commission concept is the one preferred by top producers everywhere. When it started back in the 1970s, it was controversial and widely resisted by the people who owned brokerage companies. Even now there are those who believe the 100-percent concept has ruined the industry.

Briefly, until the 100-percent-commission concept came along, top-selling real estate agents were faced with severe limitations. As some agents reached the upper echelon of the business, they found they could manage quite nicely doing little more than working with repeat customers and people who were referred to them. The problem, however, was that brokerage houses continued to take a sizable portion of agents' commission checks, while doing very little to earn them.

Historically, top producers' options were limited: They could either stay put and risk burning out on the business or leave their companies and open their own brokerage offices—complete with all the headaches and overhead of running a small business and competing against their former bosses' businesses. The net gain from going out on their own was iffy at best. And heavily factored against them was the reality that not all supersalespeople make for supermanagers.

Then along came the 100-percent-commission concept. Realty Executives to begin with, followed quickly by RE/MAX on a national scale and later Keller Williams and others, began offering top producers a third choice. Join one of their offices, keep 100 percent of whatever commissions you earned, but pay a monthly, fixed desk fee to the owner of the office to pay for rent, heating, lighting, telephones, and secretaries and, of course, to provide a profit for the owner. Desk fees today cover a wide range. A monthly fee of $1,000 or more is not unusual.

With the advent of the 100 percent commission, top producers began leaving their companies to go to the 100 percent offices, lured by the prospect of keeping more of what they earned without the headache of management. To keep their top agents, many traditional companies changed their compensation methods, creating sliding scales that allowed their best agents to keep an increasing amount of what they earned.

Clearly the 100 percent concept is not for everyone. Brand-new agents typically do not make nearly enough in the beginning to afford the monthly fees. Also, new agents usually do not join 100-percent-commission offices because there rarely is any entry-level training available. You usually gain your experience somewhere else, then move to a 100 percent office when you start making it big. And there are other drawbacks. Desk fees have to be paid, regardless of whether the market is good or bad, regardless of whether it is the homebuying season or not. Also, offices full of top producers tend to be very competitive internally, as well as externally.

But times are changing and some 100 percent offices have begun bringing in new licensees to act as assistants to the experienced agents on staff. The idea is that after several years as assistants, licensees could become agents in their own right—possibly even taking over their mentors' clients lists when the mentor agents retire.

Bill French ■

Buyer brokerage

In the old days, the cliché was, "You've got to list to live," meaning you had to list a lot of properties if you wanted to survive in the business. The notion was that if you listed lots of homes for sale, you could sit back and let all the other real estate agents in town bring their buyers to you. The more homes you listed, the better off you were.

That's still the belief in some places, but there's lots of evidence that there are other ways to make a living—and exclusive buyer brokerage is one of them. Exclusive buyer brokerage companies do not accept listings under any circumstances, specializing instead in working only with buyers. And despite what traditional companies believe, it can be lucrative.

Since the day he opened his operation in St. Louis some 25 years ago, Bill French of Wm. French Realty has never filled out a listing form, never placed a home in the multiple-listing service, never owned a "For Sale" sign, and never put a classified ad in the newspaper. Yet in a typical year he will do $80 million to $100 million in sales volume.

Laughs French, "I can tell you right now that you can get along quite nicely without taking listings."

Like some other successful real estate entrepreneurs, French has never had the desire to be in the "real estate business" per se. He considers himself to be in a service business that happens to require a real estate license.

The French company works exclusively with corporate executives and managers who are moving to the St. Louis area. Typically, purchasing the right house in the right neighborhood is only one part of an executive move. Other factors may include finding the right private school for executives' children, the right ballet class for their daughters, the right country club for their spouses, and the right riding stables for the family horses.

What a corporation doesn't want is its exectutives to move somewhere only to have their families end up so miserable that they demand to move back. That forces the corporation to not only spend another $60,000 to move its executives back, but then to find another executive to fill the open position at the second location.

French considers it his job to produce a successful relocation—not just find a house.

By business decision, French works only the buyer side of the transaction because it differentiates his company from all the other companies in town. "If you are an executive coming to St. Louis, you know that I'm going to be focused on your needs, not on my needs. By that I mean I'm not going to try to put you into a particular house just because my company has it listed and may be offering me a bonus if I sell it. I don't take listings, so you're guaranteed I'm going to show you what's on the market, regardless of who has it listed." French believes service has to come before profits, but he also believes good service will translate into good profits: A successful move of one corporate executive will often lead to handling additional moves for other company officials.

As well as working only relocation and working only the buyer side of the transaction, French also runs a focused business that benefits the bottom line of the agents who work for him.

"In my office, I'm the 'rainmaker.' I'm the one who talks to the corporate human resources people. I'm the one who goes out to the company and puts on seminars on homebuying. But when the lead comes in, I hand it over to one of the agents. They earn a split of the commission, but they have no personal marketing costs. In a traditional office, personal marketing can take a lot off an agent's bottom line. That's an expense my people don't have. The sole purpose of agents here is to service the business."

And how much can one of his agents make? Said French, "An agent here can clear above $80,000 pretty easily."

Julie Garton-Good ■

Fee-for-Service Option

A **comparatively new** idea to the real estate industry is the fee-for-service concept, which takes the commonsense but seemingly revolutionary approach that you should be paid for the work you perform and the expertise you bring to the deal, regardless of whether a real estate transaction emerges at the end.

You don't have to have been in the real estate business before you see why so many professionals like the sound of this idea. You may spend days driving a family around town looking at houses, buying their donuts, paying for their lunch, burning up your gas, and having Junior getting crumbs all over the back seat of your car. Then, suddenly, the husband will call up to say they've purchased a house through his wife's cousin. On that day, you'll understand why the idea of getting an upfront fee (and a really big one in that case) is so attractive.

The ugly truth is that almost all real estate agents give away much of their time and energy, only to have the consumers turn their backs on them. But even on a higher level, fee-for-service makes some degree of sense for both consumers and professionals.

Real estate author and educator Julie Garton-Good, author of Real Estate a la Carte (Dearborn), has developed the concept of fee-for-service to the point that she is training agents nationwide on how to charge for their time.

Says Garton-Good, "The more I explore fee-for-service, the more I realize that many people should have taken this approach when ramping up their careers instead of going in the 'spend-money-before-you-make-it' sales direction. Too many quality people are sacrificed at the altar of one-size-fits-all traditional real estate."

According to Garton-Good, new agents should consider fee-for-service if they generally fall into one of three categories:

- "Type 1: Strong specialty background, but no real estate sales experience. This could be an appraiser, a building contractor, etc. who already has services/experiences to market in an FFS [fee-for-services] approach to consumers. Unfortunately, most brokers don't know how to handle this talent and end up smashing this person into the traditional 'sales' model. The result? This person leaves the business, disheartened that he or she couldn't use his talent to make money in real estate.
- "Type 2: Combination of real-world experience and light specialty experience. A good example here might be the investor who has purchased/sold several properties, but

doesn't have (nor want to have) the sales experience to be a high-pressured salesperson. Using FFS, this person could market his/her expertise to consumers and peers alike while staying outside of the listing/selling framework.

- "Type 3: Loves the concept of real estate, but knows he or she won't be strong in sales. In fact, [someone with] this profile might even find salesmanship distasteful. Many of these people are more 'paperwork oriented' and get charged up more by contracts and detail than by salesmanship hype. Originally ostracized as 'deadwood,' this profile has now come into its own, working as profitable back-end, front-end, and personal assistant personnel. This profile will eventually be where many new agents begin in the brokerage business."

Garton-Good has created a training organization, the National Association of Real Estate Consultants (NAREC), dedicated to teaching agents how fee-for-service is done. Most agents involved with the concept say they are taking it slowly, but ironically they are finding a willing audience in the For-Sale-by-Owner market.

Agents point out that FSBOs must comply with many of the same laws that they do: They must provide honest property disclosures, and they cannot break fair housing laws. Briefing FSBOs on those issues easily could be a fee-for-service task. Likewise, many FSBOs don't really know how much to ask for their properties. A fee-for-service agent could prepare a comparative market analysis. Negotiating an offer also may be a sticking point for FSBOs that a fee-for-service agent could step into and accomplish.

A big question, of course, is how much to charge. Garton-Good's NAREC has several formulas. A number of people doing fee-for-service say they often price their hourly services at about what local attorneys charge per hour.

Another drawback, those agents add, is keeping track of the paperwork. You are, after all, a company of one person. You are going to have to do the accounting yourself and make sure the invoices go out. At some point, you may have to cut off clients who are too much in arrears.

Pat Griffin ■
Salaried agents

A **better established** cousin to fee-for-service is the salaried agent. Taking agents off commissions and putting them on fixed salaries has been tried with varying degrees of success around the country, but the idea has never really caught on in mainstream real estate. Some top people in the industry, however, believe that day may be coming soon.

Pat Griffin, who heads the relocation subsidiary of the DeWolfe Companies, based near Boston, is among those who see salaried agents as a good opportunity for the entire industry.

Griffin points out that the average age of real estate agents is now above 52, and going up. Why? Because the industry has had a hard time attracting young people to the ranks—specifically young people who are prepared to take the risk that they can support themselves from the beginning. She notes that many young people prefer employment with fixed hours and fixed salaries, and they like the idea of their employers contributing to the cost of their health benefits and life insurance and keeping track of their tax information. Most of that is not available to people in the real estate business.

Plus, to survive the early months in real estate, a new agent needs at least six months of living expenses tucked away—something very hard to do for young people. "It raises the specter that they'll have to spend six or seven more months living at home with Mom and Dad while they're trying to start their careers. That's not very appealing. Having salaried real estate agents is making more sense all the time."

What some companies also are finding is that having salaried agents—as in DeWolfe's relocation division—gives supervisors much better control over the transaction. Salaried agents can be compelled to live up to a standard set by both the corporate client and the real estate company. Independent contractors typically are not held to a specific standard, often resulting in inconsistent service. Salaried agents also can be required to attend certain training sessions that independent contractors may shrug off.

Andrew Boyd ■

Electronic brokerages

Another area where the notion of salaried agents seems to be catching on is in the new online brokerage industry, where phone calls and e-mails are fed into a central answering system and then farmed back out to the agents. Agents tend to be well paid, and they can claim to have a life outside work, as well.

Andrew Boyd, who works in the Houston office of the national franchise eRealty, moved to the new electronic side of the real estate industry after having put in more than seven years in a more traditional brokerage. "There comes a time when you see the future coming, but you're the only one in the office who does. That's when I decided it was time to move."

He had worked in an office with some 50 agents, only three of whom had Web pages and only six or seven of whom routinely used e-mail. His clients and customers, however, were substantially Web-savvy. They were surfing the Internet for homes for sale but were unable to fully exploit the benefits of the Internet because the industry was so far behind. Not infrequently, homes seen on the Net actually had been sold months before.

At eRealty, however, listings are updated throughout the day directly from the mulitple-listing service. E-mails go into a central communication center and then are fed back out to the appropriate sales associate. Questions about homes for sale in the north Houston area are routed to Boyd. If he isn't in the office or is with another client, that customer communication is then routed to another eRealty agent.

Because both Boyd and the other agents are on salary, what matters most is that the clients get served—not which agent gets the call. While Boyd is on salary, he also is eligible for bonuses based on his production. But the real question, of course, is bottom line. In his last year with his previous company, while receiving 100 percent of the commission, Boyd said he grossed about $125,000. But he had to subtract from that $1,500 per month in desk fees and another $12,000 per year in medical insurance, plus his routine business expenses. On salary at eRealty, he said he makes $50,000. But the company picks up both his gas mileage and his entertainment expenses, should he need to buy lunch for a buyer. The company also picks up part of his medical insurance and handles the normal payroll deductions for taxes and Social Security.

"I'm still a little behind where I was with the other company, but sometime in the next two years I'll easily go past what I was making there."

There are other benefits, as well.

With his former company, Boyd said, he might show clients more than 30 homes before they'd come to a purchasing decision. At eRealty, where clients are encouraged to browse the Internet and narrow their search before jumping into the agent's car, he said he typically shows only five to seven homes.

Because of its efficient use of technology, eRealty usually lists homes for 4.5 percent commissions, with 1.5 percent being the company share and the remainder going to the agent with the buyer. Being on salary, Boyd does not share in the commission split.

"I have zero regrets for leaving a bricks-and-mortar brokerage," he said. "The majority of my clients really like to do business this way. They can monitor the transaction from start to finish electronically. They don't feel hounded by an agent who is driven by commission. My clients feel more in control of the transaction. I hear that a lot. They like that."

Chapter 17

The Real Estate Business Wants You

It is believed, although not proven, that every game is winnable

For years, every personal computer delivered with Microsoft Windows has come with a small group of games that includes the ever-popular time-waster Solitaire and a much-less-noticed game called Free Cell. Free Cell also is a Solitaire-style game, in which the computer randomly deals out cards and the player must re-sort the deck into suits. It is a fairly challenging game in which the player must think many moves in advance, lest they lock up the board and have the computer declare, "Sorry, you lose." The "Help" section of Free Cell offers very little assistance to the player, but it does make one intriguing observation: "It is believed, although not proven, that every game is winnable."

That can be said of much of life, and it certainly can be said of the real estate business today. To paraphrase just a little: It is believed, although not proven, that anybody can be a success in this industry. The doors of the American real estate industry are wide open to you. Real estate is, in fact, one of the few businesses left in this country where an expensive diploma from a lofty business school is hardly a necessity. Not only that, but a big-time degree from a big-time university is hardly a harbinger of a big-time income.

Tom Dallas ■

Dropping Out to the Top

The career of Tom Dallas is a good example. In 1979, Dallas found his way into the real estate business in the San Francisco. He had dropped out of high school years earlier to help run his family's restaurant business, and then moved in the savings and loan business, ending up managing the largest S&L in San Francisco. His lack of formal education hardly stopped him from achieving success. Today, Dallas is a top-selling agent in the worldwide Coldwell Banker real estate system. He had more than $300 million in sales in 2000, and in the course of his career he has sold more than $1 billion worth of real estate.

For him there were three keys to getting started: A yellow legal pad, simply knowing more about the neighborhoods in his community than anybody else on the face of the earth, and passion. "You have to like what you are doing, and I have a passion for real estate."

"When I started out, I made a list of all the people I knew. And I graded them A, B, or C. An 'A' was an immediate buyer or seller, somebody who had a need to do something today. 'B' was somebody who was looking, who didn't have to make a decision today, but who would make a decision today if all the right ingredients were there. 'C' was a back burner: People who are hard to pin down on what they want. Or they know what they want but have a ridiculous price in mind." As he continued to meet people during open houses, while doing floor time, or even at social events, he would continue to add to his contact list. "I'd look at it every day, and I'd talk to people. Some people would go from an A to a C, or from a C to a B. Over time the list got larger and larger."

As the list grew and as he sat more open houses, his knowledge of the San Francisco peninsula region grew. And he took every opportunity to share that information with his clients and customers. "When people come into an open house, you want to display your knowledge. You want them to know that you know more about your area than anybody else. If this house doesn't fit their needs, you want to be able to cite four other properties that you know are on the market or will be coming onto the market."

Dallas remembers getting into the business just as mortgage interest rates were hitting 16, 17, and 18 percent. The market was coming to a halt, and the sky was filled with agents bailing out of the business. Dallas managed to gain a toehold, however. The most important element both then and now, he says, was his ability to explain to his clients what was happening in their transactions and convey a feeling of trust. "If people feel you are treating them consistently and ethically correct, they come back and work with you again. Pretty soon, they start giving your number to their friends."

Today, Dallas feels nobody knows more about his sales territory—which he refers to as "dirt"—than he does. "I love dirt," he says. "I'm king of dirt. I know where the best properties are. I know the best locations. I honestly feel nobody knows this area like I do." An important note to add about Dallas is that he's also managed to keep his life together. Unlike more than a few other real estate professionals, he has been able to balance his professional life and his personal life. He has been married for 23 years, but concedes that when he was first getting started, hard choices had to be made.

"At one point several years ago, I looked at all the people on top of the industry, all the top real estate agents in our area, and not one of them was still married. I didn't want that to happen to me. You want to be at home with your family, but sometimes the phone rings at 2 or 3 or 4 o'clock in the morning. There are no leads that a young real estate agent won't follow up on. I'm older and a lot wiser now. You sort through those things. You need to find a way to have privacy if you are going to survive with your family."

And he adds this note: "You need to have energy to be really good [at real estate]. Not everybody should be in this business."

Now, even more than when Dallas came into the business, real estate has become a welcome haven for entrepreneurs—of any education, any race, any religion, any national origin—who are willing to work hard to make a living. In real estate, the elevator to success goes all the way to the top. There are no signs that say, "Only well-educated white men beyond this point."

But make no mistake. There is nothing altruistic about real estate companies recruiting minorities. There certainly is nothing do-gooder about it. It is a matter of profits. In the United States today, the vast majority of real estate license holders are white Americans, and the vast majority of home owners also are white. To the industry, that poses both a problem and an opportunity wrapped up in a single question: Can the industry profit if it can raise the home ownership level among nonwhites? As African Americans, Hispanic Americans, and people of other races, religions, and national origins make significant strides in economic clout, the answer clearly is "yes."

But if research has proven anything over the decades, it is that consumers prefer to make their purchases—from 10-cent candy to $1-million homes—from people they can identify with. With America being such a melting pot, that means an increasing need for all kinds of people in every conceivable profession, with real estate high on the list.

Even as a new agent, if you were to look around just a little, you would see evidence that real estate is a place where imagination, ingenuity, and sheer chutzpah not only are welcome but sometimes even thrive. Several Internet sites have now opened specifically for the purpose of assisting gay homebuyers. An increasing number of older Americans are turning to people their own age to help them with living choices as they retire from the working world to a more leisurely lifestyle. Disabled Americans also have real estate Web sites catering to their housing needs.

For the past several decades, African Americans have been able to turn to the National Association of Real Estate Brokers (NAREB), a predominantly African American group of real estate professionals, to help them with their homebuying and selling requirements. Also, relatively new but already growing in strength, the National Association of Hispanic Real Estate Professionals is a resource for both Hispanic American con sumers and Hispanic Americans who already are inside the industry.

M a r t y   R o d r i g u e z ■
Taking the Job Seriously

Perhaps the greatest irony is, however, that no matter what race, religion, national origin, or other subset new sales associates fit into, they all seem to have the same problems.

"If I had several brand-new sales associates sitting in my office, the first thing I'd say to them is, 'Take this job seriously,'" says Marty Rodriguez.

Rodriguez, a Hispanic American born in Los Angeles, is a perfect example of the face that real estate has no ceiling, glass or otherwise. She has climbed the ladder of real estate success to become the top-selling agent in the world's largest real estate organization, the Century 21 franchise. She has even trademarked her name.

For the past few decades she has worked largely with the Hispanic community, but her clientele today is about 50 percent Hispanic. The rest cut across a broad spectrum. Her complaint about new sales associates, however, could be heard in any office, anywhere in the country.

"So many people who get their licenses do not take the job seriously and pretty soon they fail. They don't seem to understand what real estate can do for them." She also adds, however, that there are many brokers and company owners whose attitudes are no better than those of their sales associates. "They don't take it seriously, either. They don't train their people properly. They do very little to help new people into the business." And usually the result is the same: New sales associates depart before they really get started.

"New people—no matter how old they are—need to know they don't have to be the youngest or the prettiest person in the office to do well in this business. But they do need to come to work every day with a fresh attitude. I know people in their 20s who are 'old,' and I know people in their 90s who are never going to be old. The right attitude makes all the difference."

Those with the wrong attitude, she says, are "energy vampires." "I've worked in other offices where the energy vampires will come in and drink the coffee. They complain about the market and why they can't sell anything. The interest rates are too high, or the market is bad. They suck the energy right out of the office. You have to stay away from those people."

Rodriguez was educated at a Catholic girls' school in Los Angeles, and took some additional courses at a junior college. While she believes a formal education is good to have, there are other important factors in being a top sales associate. "The more education you have, the better you will be at business," she says. "It's not the only thing, but it's going to help you. It gives you a better position." Of far more import, however, are "people skills." "If you know your business—*really* know your business—people won't care where you're from or what you look like."

Rodriguez is a demanding employer who insists that her associates maintain high standards. She is the only listing agent in the office. Her daughter is the broker in charge. Rodriguez has eight other agents she works with in the office, all of whom are buyer agents. "Everyone in my office knows the contract like the back of their hand. You learn the purchase agreement so if there ever is a question, you know what the answer is. I have seen too many agents from other companies be asked questions about the contract, and they either can't answer or they guess. There are liability issues involved. It is very scary. My name is on this company and my reputation is on the line whenever [associates] go out. They have to know the contract."

She expects her agents to caravan neighborhoods and view new listings on a daily basis, and unlike many companies, she also continues to require that her agents make cold calls. "That's one reason why so many [new sales associates] are unsuccessful. If you don't talk to people, if you aren't trying to make contacts, how else are you going to get business? If the person on the other end of the phone says, 'No,' or hangs up on you, that's no big deal. You go on to the next."

Rejection, she says, is part of the real estate business. "You shouldn't be in the business if you can't handle rejection. You don't have to like it, but you have to get used to it. I used to make cold calls and I hated to do it. But it was the only way I knew to get my business to the next level. For new agents, four days a week they must be on the phone for at least an hour or two a day."

She also insists that everything be put in writing, especially when working with agents outside her company. "Some of these agents talk in circles," she says. "They want this, or they'll give up something. As soon as my agent gets back to the office, I have them put it in writing and send it over to the other agent. 'This is to confirm that we talked about this and here's what we decided to do . . . ' We do everything in writing. There is too much at stake." Rodriguez also cautions new agents against trying to find a niche too early in their careers. "I remember in 1989, there were a lot of people who just wanted to work the upper end of the market. Well, the market turned and those houses stopped selling. Those agents were out of the business in no time."

Heeding her own warning, the Rodriguez company works all kinds of homes, from below $100,000 to well over $1 million. "Our average sale is probably about $240,000."

On the personal side, Rodriguez warns that the intensity of real estate can kill family relationships. "People tend to marry a person who either brings out the best in you or takes it away. I have always had great support from my husband and my children. I've seen a lot of great real estate agents who don't have that, and it ends up affecting their business.

"To be successful in real estate, you need to make a commitment to it. That means your family has to make a commitment, too."

Chapter 18

You and the Gurus of Salesmanship

When do you know enough to know that you need to know more?

A s you've probably already heard, it's true that even after you have your license, you are never out of school in the real estate business. What also is true, however, is that your educational needs are about to take two different paths—one is required by your state government, the other is demanded by your bank account.

Briefly, here's what you need to know about the state path: For as long as you have your license, there are going to be continuing education (CE) requirements that you will need to meet every few years. These CE hours, of course, are mandated to keep your license current. And, in the greater sense of protecting the public—that is, protecting consumers from you—they really are a good idea.

Mandated CE will deal with a wide range of subjects, probably including something about contracts; something about the newest wrinkle in agency law; almost certainly something about ethics, trust accounts, and mandatory property disclosures. All those issues are in play in almost every state in the nation. The state and the public want you to know what's going on. And even if you wanted to live in ignorance, you're not going to have that option.

The education path that deals with your bank account is far more fun and far more interesting. Here is where you are going to meet the gurus of real estate salesmanship: the men and women who can help build your career from the nothing you're producing today to the great big something you can produce tomorrow.

But wait a minute, you say, isn't my supervising broker supposed to teach me about all this? Isn't my company supposed to train me? The answer is yes, of course, in a perfect world that's how it would be. In the real world, however, your supervisor may be trying to keep track of 100 sales agents, so how much time is going to be spent on you? That's why you need to find your personal guru.

Going to Your Guru

After you've been in the business for a while—and a very short while at that—you will start receiving helpful announcements about all sorts of courses that are available to help you make money. These salesmanship, or "professional development," courses are designed to give you a different angle on your competitors, or provide one more idea that could lead to two more closings per year—or maybe 10 more, or 20.

The longer you stay in the business the more names you are going to hear, names like Tom Hopkins, Joe Klock, Danielle Kennedy, Howard Brinton, Terri Murphy, David Knox, David Beson, Rand Smith, and on and on. All these people are sales trainers—people who have been in your shoes, who have been successful, and now are in the business of helping you become successful.

The vast majority of them are very knowledgeable, very insightful, and quite frankly they are usually very entertaining. The secret of being a successful real estate speaker is to be experienced, service-oriented, positive, and preferably, a performer. Actually, those aren't bad rules for being a successful real estate *agent*, either. Most of the people mentioned above and many others travel coast-to-coast giving seminars on subjects such as how to improve your listing presentations, how to get your buyers to make decisions, and how to get the most out of your online marketing programs, and so forth.

A lot of these people also have developed "personal coaching" programs where you can—for a fee—talk to them on a weekly or monthly basis. Depending on how much you pay, and it could range from a few hundred dollars to more than a thousand per year, you'll be able to talk about what you're doing right, what you're doing wrong, and get some suggestions on what you might want to do next.

Do they help? Like so much in real estate, the answer is both yes and no. There are two parts to any communication: the talking side and the listening side. There are some coaches you'll "hear" better than others. You'll be more comfortable with their message and their style, and you'll find a ring of truth in what they say. Until you find that particular coach, your personal guru, none of them will work very well for you.

As a practical matter, though, keep in mind that just about every top producer quoted in this book had a mentor of some kind, some kind of "coach" who inspired them to take their business to the next level.

So when the opportunities arise and these sales trainers bring their traveling road shows to a town near you, you should go hear what they have to say. A good way to "sample" a lot of trainers is by going to professional conventions. When you find one you like, sign up.

So When Do You Do It?

That's a good question. At what point in your real estate career do you want to get involved with sales trainers? There is no universal correct answer, but generally speaking, if you have a chance to catch a seminar on your first day of work, and it's free or inexpensive, then you should probably go. Otherwise, however, you're going to have a hard time justifying the expense until you've been in the business awhile.

Most sales trainers talk about real-life experiences they've had calling on clients and customers. They have dialogues they like you to use; special letters they've already drafted that you can sign and send out to your client list; special ways to deal with objections, rejections, and problems. For the most part, you're not going to understand what they're talking about until you've done a few deals, been to a few closings, had the experience of showing buyers property, and generally had a few objections, rejections, and problems of your own.

Following the Curve

Some trainers believe agents should wait at least until they've gone through their company training program before they seek out sales trainers. They argue that if you're just a little way into the learning curve and if you haven't really started working with some of the productivity software, then it's not going to be worth your time. But you want to start thinking about trainers before you get into some bad habits, often not more than a couple of months after you begin work.

A good trainer can be a gold mine for sales associates, doing everything from giving you a kick in the butt to get you going all the way to giving you an entire system in which all you have to do is follow the directions.

Terri Murphy ■

Working from a Script

Terri Murphy, a broker, author, and trainer from Chicago, points out that trainers can provide their clients actual scripts to be memorized that cover every aspect of marketing, from what to say in a cold call to what to say in a listing presentation. Some packages provide specific letters to be sent to your sphere-of-influence list, and include language for follow-up postcards and phone calls. They may even provide a schedule to tell you when to send out a card, how many weeks you should wait until you send out another one, and so forth. Every script, every letter, and every postcard has been developed for the purpose of making the sale.

Says Murphy, "I think all of us have tested these letters and scripts a thousand times ourselves. It doesn't really make any sense for new agents to try to develop their own marketing materials. They shouldn't have to be their own copy editors or direct-mail houses when resources are available that do all that for you."

Dave Beson ■

Systematic Sales

Dave Beson, from Minneapolis, believes new sales associates need to move toward customized sales systems as soon as they arrive in the industry. "You have people who are working in jobs making $3,000 per month, and they are thinking about going into real estate. They think they'll try it for a couple of months and see if they're any good at it. So they save up some money so they can live for two or three months. But they don't want to spend any extra money on training. They think they can figure out the real estate business on their own. So after three months they've got nothing to show for it. They've spent their savings and they have to go back to another job.

"It would have been smarter for them to have taken one month's salary–$3,000–and invested it immediately in getting themselves set up in the business. For that much money you can get some low-tech business cards, a database service for mass mailing, and you can invest in some training so you'll know what to say when you actually do get someone on the phone." Beson says the sales trainers currently out there working with agents know what gets results because most of them made tens of thousands of presentations themselves when they were agents. "We've seen it all before, we've heard it all before." What Beson finds most curious is that most sales associates worry about their careers in exactly reverse order.

"They start by focusing on the dollars. They start by saying, 'I really need some money.' After they worry about that for a while, they figure out, 'What I really need is a transaction. I've got to get a transaction.' After they worry about that for a while, they start saying, 'If I could just get a listing, I'd be OK. If I could just get a listing.' Then pretty soon, they start saying, 'I need an appointment. If I could just get an appointment, I could get things going.' Next thing they start saying is, 'I'd settle for a lead. If I just had a lead.'

"That," says Beson, "brings them to where they should have started in the first place. They should have started with prospecting for leads—and that's what sales trainers help you do. They help you develop systems that prospect for leads."

Those who worry about their business in the right order, he says, tend to have less to worry about in general.

Roger Turcotte ■

Negotiation Makes or Breaks the Deal

But while most cross-country speakers focus on bringing the business in the front door, relatively few actually go into the art of closing the deal once the buyer and seller have begun making offers and counteroffers. In a world where most of the time you don't get paid unless the deal closes, it is trainers like Roger Turcotte of Contoocook, New Hampshire, a specialist in how to negotiate, who become of critical importance. And his *is* the kind of training that new sales associates need from the beginning.

Says Turcotte, "Negotiation is the unsung hero of a successful real estate career." Turcotte argues that sales agents can draw on negotiating skills throughout the day, every day, whether trying to get a higher commission split from the owner of the company or trying to get a deal closed on time and with everyone smiling at the end.

In real estate, Turcotte notes, negotiating takes two basic forms of equal importance:

1. Negotiating *on your own behalf.* You negotiate on your own behalf when you are sitting across from a potential client during a listing presentation. As you discuss and defend your commission, you essentially are negotiating your salary.

2. Negotiating *on your client's behalf.* Here you are an observer, acting as an adviser to your client on the decisions he or she has to make that affect the deal.

As a participant in negotiations, he says, you take risks based on the rewards available to you. "When I'm face-to-face with a seller, and he wants to give me a listing contract for 90 days and I think I'm going to need 120 days to sell the house, I need to figure out what my risks are. Do I want to spend the money advertising the listing if I've only got it for 90 days? Do I want to put my energy into it if I really think it won't sell in that time? You need to be able to assess those kinds of questions."

Alternatively, when working with a client, you need to be able to assess the risks the client is taking as he or she goes into the deal. And you need to remember that you are not just talking about financial risks; you are talking about emotional risks, as well. "A lot of things have to come out of a successful closing," Turcotte says. "There's the financial side—but there's also the emotional side." And the emotional side can be very tricky, indeed.

Like Walking on Hot Coals

In the bad old days before there were such things as buyer agents, home inspections, and property disclosures, once a purchase agreement was reached and the financing arranged, the deal was done. Today, however, some buyers and their agents consider the purchase price only another step in the ongoing negotiating process.

Contracts are tied down by contingencies, and buyers often use those contingencies to reopen negotiations on price. The purchase agreement may be set at $290,000, but when the roof inspector finds the shingles need to be replaced, suddenly the buyer is back at the table looking for a $10,000 reduction in price.

Likewise, buyers may not be able to close on the property until they sell their current house. Such a contingency may make a seller reluctant to offer any price concessions at all.

"Unfortunately, a lot of buyer agents out there feel they're not doing their job unless they rake the seller over the coals. The problem with that," says Turcotte, "is that if you rake the seller over the coals, you've raked the seller over the coals. When the time comes that you need a little flexibility or a problem arises on your side of the table, there isn't going to be any give by the seller."

Turcotte has seen closings where there has been so much animosity that there had to be two rooms, one for the buyers and the other for the sellers, with the closing officer walking the paperwork back and forth for signatures. There have been closings where a seller has refused to come to the closing and just told their attorney to handle it.

Such anger can spread far beyond the closing table, Turcotte points out, especially in smaller towns where everyone knows everyone else—where the buyer's son could end up on the seller's Little League team, or the seller could be forced to take his car to the buyer's auto shop. "The best defense against problems," says Turcotte, "is make sure there are no surprises." Starting with the listing presentation, Turcotte recommends not only that you and your sellers discuss your marketing plan for their home but that you begin advising them about what will happen once offers start coming in.

"When there is an offer on the table and an issue comes up, your best advice to the seller may be to be flexible on that question. But sometimes that seller is going to turn on you and say, 'Well, you just want us to take it so you can get your commission.' That's the point when you need to remind them that, 'No, you remember we discussed this possibility before. We agreed this is how we'd handle it.'"

Likewise, on the buyer side of the deal, you should walk your clients through the negotiating process even before they select a home, again with the hope of blunting the impact of surprises.

Turcotte reminds us, however, that politeness is never out of style, and that a client always has the right to change his mind. "You always have to remember that you're the adviser here. It's not your decision to make."

Professional Parenting

As you gain experience in your real estate career, you will hear stories, and maybe even participate in stories, of good, solid, intelligent deals that are blown apart because buyers and sellers and buyer agents and listing agents didn't know how to cross the final gap in their negotiating positions.

"Buyers come in with low-ball offers, and you have to tell them, 'I've got to warn you that this offer could be considered an insult by the sellers and they may not counter. By law, Mr. Buyer, I have to present this offer and I will, but you have to understand there is a risk if you really want the house.'"

On the seller side, he says, listing agents need to remind sellers that sometimes buyers make offers on what they "need," not on what they "get." "Maybe it's more house than the buyer really thinks he needs. His price is going to be based on how much he's willing to spend for a house the size that he needs, not a house that's the size he's going to get. The listing agent needs to understand that and make his explanation to the sellers. That's going to help the sellers decide how to make a counteroffer."

Turcotte believes teenagers are probably the best negotiators on the planet and that real estate agents could learn a lot about negotiating from dealing with their children."Maybe your kid wants to borrow the car or have an extension on his curfew, and you say OK. But then the next week you may want him to clean out the garage, and he says 'No.' And you say, 'Wait a minute. Remember last week when I let you take the car?' The teenager sees these things as separate events. They don't see them as being tied together."

The same thing can happen when you're negotiating for a house. Your buyer client may be reluctant, but finally agree to pay the $300,000 listing price. Then, three weeks later, after an inspection turns up termite damage, the buyer might come back to the seller and ask for a $10,000 reduction in price. If the seller says, "No," the buyer is going to feel like he's been had. The reality, says Turcotte, is that those are separate events unless you link them early in the transaction process."Terms and conditions need to be set at the beginning, otherwise people are going to get this sense of indebtedness," Turcotte says. "Terms and conditions have to be clear from the beginning."

Turcotte says it takes time to develop the skills of a negotiator, but it's also worthwhile. Real estate negotiation is a question of "process" and "results," and people tend to remember both.

Consumers who get what they want from a deal but feel like they've been roughed up in the process will rarely go back to the same sales associate who let it happen, nor will they refer friends. Remember that.

Chapter 19

To Tech, or Not To Tech?

Actually, that's not really a question

Here's a bit of good news. You're in real estate at a perfect time—at least a perfect time in terms of the technology you need to get the job done in today's world. If you had started yesterday, you would have been way too early. Had you waited until tomorrow, you'd have been way too late. But today is technologically perfect. And here's even more good news: Because you started today, you are a perfect fit for the real estate industry of the future, arguably even better than the agents around you. Boy, are we glad you finally got here.

This is a good time for you to be entering this business because chances are that you're familiar with many of the high-tech ideas that are changing real estate as most of us know it. Agents who entered the business as little as five years ago are still struggling with a lot of these changes.

For instance, if you just recently got out of school, you've probably already spent a lot of time surfing the Web, doing research, and learning how to navigate the Internet so that you can get what you need with some degree of efficiency. Agents who have been in real estate awhile have had to learn all those things from scratch, and they usually have had to pay someone to help them learn.

Alternatively, if you've come from another line of work, there is a good possibility that you've used computers before, that you know what an application is, that you've likely done some word processing and maybe even been involved in some spreadsheet accounting programs. You may have worked with databases of customer lists—maybe even mail-merge programs. None of these experiences will be wasted, now that you're in real estate.

OK, you're saying, but how does that put me ahead of anyone else? The lament is that real estate has had a hard time reconciling itself to the computer age. Keep in mind that the vast majority of today's sales associates are only doing a couple of deals a year. They haven't yet seen the need to invest money in things like computers and e-mail programs, let alone acquire the training to really make those gadgets pay for themselves. On top of that, you have thousands of agents who are convinced tomorrow will never come, who argue, "This is how I do it, this is how I've always done it, and I see no need to change." What those agents—yesterday's top producers—haven't realized is that the consumer has changed, even if the agent hasn't.

The first step on the road to a successful sales career is to be a member of the same culture as your clients. And most of your clients already are part of the technology culture.

Industry statistics show that even among real estate agents who have e-mail addresses, more than 50 percent check their e-mail only a couple of times a week, and many don't respond to e-mail for five days or more. In today's world, of course, where consumers have many choices and many people are competing for their business, a sales associate who doesn't respond to an e-mail inquiry within 24 hours runs a serious risk of losing business to someone who responds within 8 hours—and four hours is even better.

So, again, the good news is that you probably already are more technologically fit for the future than many of the people who have been working in your office for years. The bad news is that, as a new sales associate, you don't have enough money or experience to really make a big technosplash.

But back to the good-news side, maybe you don't have to make a really big splash, at least in the beginning.

B r u c e   B e n h a m ■

Technology Realities

Bruce **Benham, the** technology guru at RE/MAX International, works with multimillion-dollar systems, oversees interactive Web sites that fit somewhere between technology and magic, and at one time or another has probably pushed every new button on every new gadget that Intel's nerds have designed.

Yet, what does he recommend for new agents? "Well, they need to have access to a computer somewhere, either at home or at the office. A cell phone is a 'must have.' And you need to make sure it comes with voice mail. You need to have an e-mail address. Preferably not an America Online address. But it's better than nothing."

What about a pager? A Palm computer? What about a Web site? Shrugs Benham, "Not when you're first starting out." Pagers, he says, are virtually obsolete, replaced by multi-talented cell phones that seem to do more and more all the time. Handheld computing devices are certainly nice, he says, but "that's really a second-tier thing. It's something you have to have when you've reached the next level, but not when you're starting out. In the beginning, you're not going to have a lot of appointments to keep track of. And you're not going to have that many phone numbers. That's something that can wait."

And a Web page? Benham believes that certainly if your company offers you a page on the corporate Web site, you should take it. But the problem is, if you're new in the business, what are you going to put on it? You're not a top producer (yet). You probably don't have any profound insights into the business (yet). You are not lofty enough to pronounce company policy, and you may not even be able to post a literate (let alone legitimate) argument on why consumers should choose you as their agent instead of someone else.

Says Benham, "Web sites are important, but they are more important to sellers than they are to buyers. Sellers want to make sure they know where to go on the Internet to view their property . . . and they want to know where else it's going to be on the Internet. But as a practical matter, most new real estate agents are going to be working with buyers. On the buyer side, Web sites aren't that important." There is, of course, some disagreement on how technological you need to be, and how soon.

Terri Murphy ■

Get on the Web—*Now*

Broker, author, and lecturer Terri Murphy, one of the nation's top speakers on the need for real estate agents to gear up on technology, believes even the newest agent needs a Web presence from Day 1. Murphy, whose book *e-listing and e-selling secrets* (Dearborn, 2001) has become a bible for the e-commerce side of the real estate business, believes Web sites are an important weapon in every agent's marketing arsenal. Murphy suggests that even if you just put up a page that says, "JOHN SMITH'S REAL ESTATE SITE IS UNDER CONSTRUCTION," you've at least demonstrated to your potential clients that you understand the need to be on the Web. She reasons that today's consumers expect their agent to have a cell phone, e-mail, and a Web site. Even if the site is not aggressive in sending a positive message, she argues, the lack of any site at all sends a very negative message. Even more to the point, she says, your own personal Web site, whose address appears on your business cards; your stationery; and every piece of marketing material that you distribute is another step toward establishing you as your own brand name.

"You absolutely have to market yourself. You have to market you even as you market the company," she says. "Look, your clients are never going to meet Mr. Coldwell or Mr. Banker. They may never meet your broker, and they'll probably never meet the owner of the company. You're the one your clients are dealing with. You're the name that has to be out front."

A decent Web site, she maintains, is another tool that keeps your name out there. She recommends you have your own domain name, such as "MarySmith.com" or "MarySellsRealEstate.net." Domain names are fairly inexpensive if you shop around—as little as

$54 for two years. On top of that, you need to have a company host your site—figure a minimum of a couple of hundred dollars per year. And, you'll either need someone to design a site, which can be costly, or you can buy a software program and do it yourself. Web design software programs can run from fairly cheap, at about $50, to all the way up to $400 or more. For new agents, costs do add up quickly, so price out everything before you actually take the plunge. Talk to your supervising broker or a top producer in the office to make sure this is a direction where you want to go from the very beginning.

If you are leaning against investing in a Web site, Murphy likes to point out that even when you're not out there selling yourself, your Web site can be. "It's there to serve your clients 24 hours a day, 7 days a week," she says. But, she also emphasizes, you have to keep a Web site up-to-date with fresh information because you want to give the people on your sphere-of-influence list a reason to keep coming back. "A good Web site needs to be 'self-serving,'" she says. "But it needs to be self-serving for your clients, not for you."

To that end, Murphy suggests posting things like, "Seven ways to prepare your home for sale" or "Five ways to get the mortgage you want." Articles need to be informative and useful for your consumers. Articles on such topics and more already exist and, in fact, are available to Web sites from a variety of vendors. (If you have nothing else to put on your site, at the end of this chapter there is a starter content package entitled "11 Tips for a Successful Open House." Feel free to put that list on your site. No charge.)

M i c h a e l   R u s s e r ■

"Mr. Internet"

The question of whether you really need a Web site from Day 1 is far from being resolved. Michael Russer, who calls himself "Mr. Internet" and lectures nationwide on the virtue of the Web, suggests brand-new real estate agents probably don't need a Web site until they've been in the business for at least six months. "New agents are so busy learning the ropes and just figuring out how the industry works that having a Web site would be more of a burden to them than a help. And if you're going to get involved in technology," he emphasizes, "you need to get some training on how to make everything work together. I don't think you should do that until you've got a couple of transactions under your belt. I don't even know if you'd understand it before then."

If you do decide to get involved in the Internet early in your career, do keep in mind a couple of Russer's rules of the road:

- Don't send e-mail to people you don't have a working relationship with. People get angry if you send them unsolicited e-mail, commonly known as *spam*.
- Don't attach anything to a file unless you've told the person on the end that you're sending an attachment. Attachments, such as photos or forms can take forever to download. If the person on the receiving end doesn't know the attachment is coming, they are just as likely to delete the whole message.
- Be sure to put the communication basics on all business emails: your name, your phone number, your company name. You may be required by state law to put in your broker's name, as well. Check with your supervising broker.

Make no mistake, eventually you are going to want a presence on the Web.

Judy McCutchin ■

Being Web-Smart

If you do decide to go with a Web site early in your career, a good one to take a look at is www.dallashomes.com, posted by RE/MAX real estate associate Judy McCutchin. You'll notice a lot of features that enhance the visitor's experience, as well as a dog named "Chester" you can chat with.

What you won't see is a lot about RE/MAX or much red, white, and blue—the franchise's colors. And perhaps even more interesting is the role that Chester plays. McCutchin doesn't brag about her own abilities in real estate; she leaves that to the animated dog. But more important, does it work? McCutchin does about $35 million in volume every year. Roughly a third of that, more than $15 million, is directly traceable to the Web site.

But even she says, "If you're just starting out, you do not have to spend thousands of dollars. In the past several years real estate agents have spent millions of dollars on Web sites, and as far as I'm concerned, most of it has been just wasted." What should a new agent do?

Says McCutchin, "There are a lot of good, inexpensive Web site templates out there that will get you going just fine. I think you need some kind of minimal site early in your career, but it doesn't have to be expensive and it doesn't have to do a lot."

More important for new agents, she said, is mastering e-mail and knowing how to get the most out of the computer programs you have. "The best advice I can give a new agent is, 'Spend a little time and little money to get some education first about the Internet and the Web. Understand how you can use it to market yourself.'

"Understand that marketing on the Web is different from other kinds of real estate marketing. A lot of real estate marketing is 'in your face' marketing. But when you're marketing on the Web, remember that the consumer is in control. It's a very soft sell on the Web. First the consumer is going to get to know your site, then maybe they'll get to know you. If you push them, they'll be gone in a second."

But the last word on the subject has to come from those thousands of real estate agents who have invested a lot of money on a Web presence. That reminder is that there are, after all, no houses on the Internet. Web sites and e-mail are great tools, but they are not a substitute for meeting clients face-to-face and talking to them over a cup of coffee. No matter what you think of the Internet, real estate is a personal communication business, and it's going to be that way for a long time. And for heaven's sake, if you find yourself talking on the phone to someone who might want to do business with you, don't ever answer their questions by saying, "You know, all that information is on my Web site." Although you know how easy and efficient that is, it's the same thing as dismissing potential business with the words, "You're not important enough to me to talk to personally. Deal with my Web site."

If you find yourself on the phone with a confused consumer, the best thing you can possibly do is answer their questions (even if they are on the Web site) in the most friendly manner you can, and then thank them for calling you. Not everybody is comfortable with dealing with technology. And, in fact, a lot of people still prefer to deal directly with a human being. Personally helping a consumer, even ones you don't know, is always worth your time. You never know where business is going to come from.

---

11 Tips for a Successful Open House

Here are 11 ideas to help make your home more attractive to potential buyers.

1. **The outside must shine.** You'd be surprise at how many buyers "sell themselves" on your house on the basis of their first impression as they drive up the street. It's called *curb appeal*. You can enhance curb appeal by making sure the lawn is mowed, the bushes are trimmed, and the flower beds are freshly mulched. Spending a few hundred dollars on fresh paint on the front of the house can return thousands of dollars in sale price. Especially touch up the trim.

2. **The inside must look new.** Again, paint is cheap. Be your own worst critic. If you think a room could be brightened with a fresh coat of paint, do it.

3. **Make cosmetic repairs.** Windows that are cracked, holes in the walls, and tiles that are chipped all send the wrong message to a potential buyer. Things you may tend to overlook on a daily basis are the things buyers seize on. The buyer is going to assume that if there are many flaws that can be seen, then there may be even more serious flaws that can't be seen.

4. **Let in as much light as possible.** Open all the curtains. Turn on all the lights in the house (even in the middle of the day) and increase the wattage in the lightbulbs of all the lamps.

5. **Get rid of the clutter.** Don't just stash it somewhere, get it off the premises. Remember, every room in the house has to be available for inspection and every room needs to shout to a homebuyer, "There's plenty of room here for your stuff!"

6. **Set the dinner table as if you are getting ready for a dinner party.** Put out your best china and silverware. Put out your best glasses. Don't forget the candles. In this room, and in every room, the idea is to show potential buyers how they would live in your home… that it's a place where they'll be happy to entertain their guests.

7. **Kitchens and bathrooms absolutely must be spotless.** Shelves and countertops must be clean and well organized. Also, assume that people will be looking through your medicine cabinet. If there is anything there you don't want on public display, get rid of it. Same for inside cabinets and drawers.

8. **Remove some of your possessions.** Again, the idea is to make your home look as roomy as possible. If the house is packed floor to ceiling with your possessions, it makes it harder for potential buyers to see how they'd live in the house.

9. **Put your pets somewhere else.** Dogs especially are a problem and must be moved somewhere else, preferably to another part of town. Seriously. Why? Because when strangers come into a house, your dog may very well start barking. You don't want the dog to interfere with the buyer's ability to see the house. But don't ask your neighbor to keep the dog during the open house, either. If your dog senses there are strangers wandering through your house, it may start barking from next door. That will make potential buyers think the neighbors have a loud dog, and that could be a real turnoff.

10. **Bad smells kill deals.** It is worth your money to make sure your house is clean and odor free. Pet smells, urine on carpets, cigarette smoke, things you don't even notice anymore will attack the senses of visitors. Use air fresheners if need be. The old standby is to bake cookies or bread to send an inviting aroma throughout the house.

11. **Leave.** Yes, you. As soon as I arrive to supervise your open house, you should pack the kids in the car and go somewhere. We want potential buyers to freely walk around your home and see everything they want to see without you looking over their shoulders. Once you have prepared your home for the open house, leave it up to me to handle the rest.

Chapter 20

Practice Good Habits

*The business is tough enough, don't help by
self-destructing*

I n real estate, like most other enterprises, good habits lead to good business and bad habits lead to poor business, and maybe even no business at all. It's a difficult job under the best of conditions, and it doesn't help if you fall into professional—or unprofessional—habits that lead to self-destruction. It goes without saying that some people probably shouldn't get licenses in the first place. Maybe they don't have the right attitude; maybe they don't have the right temperament. Maybe they don't have the right focus or enough patience. Those people tend to work their way out of the industry in a relatively short time.

More tragic, however, are the number of sales associates who seem to get off to a good start and seem to be enjoying the business, but then hit a rough stretch and quite literally don't know how to recover. What those new associates don't realize is that even top producers hit slumps. The major difference is that top producers have the confidence and the knowledge—and, OK, the money—to do what it takes to get back on the right path. They know whom to call and whom to talk to. New agents usually have neither confidence nor knowledge, and certainly not enough money, to pull themselves back out of a slump. An early exit is the result.

And what makes matters even worse is that in real estate, a whole career can change in a matter of days—sometimes a matter of hours—and often because of events that people have no control over. But change is not always a bad thing: An unfriendly, unproductive atmosphere in an office can turn around in a heartbeat if an office manager is suddenly replaced. Sometimes, even the departure of a top producer can bring new life into an otherwise stagnant office.

Likewise, some sales programs just take awhile to kick in. The calls you make and the cards you send out today may not pay off for 18 months. Nobody knows why a sales strategy doesn't work the way it's supposed to. Nobody knows why a particular customer will remember your name so many months after your initial introduction. Who knows how long your card will sit on someone's refrigerator before that someone actually makes a call? It's a strange business that way. And, of course, the fear always is that the phone won't start ringing for you until the day after you decide to give up.

As we've seen, many of the nation's most productive real estate agents had only meager sales their first year in the business, so immediate success obviously is not a sign of long-term well-being. Sometimes you just have to stick with it.

Sometimes careers take off, then go dead, and then take off again. Various sales gurus have various explanations for why this happens, but ultimately what it comes down to is a mix of bad habits and bad luck. But as more sales managers around the country become more attuned to the events that can lead to sales agent failure, they are finding that if you can change bad habits, you often can change bad luck. So, as you evaluate your career path in the months and years ahead, it might be worthwhile to keep some of these checkpoints in mind.

Feed the Front End

Failing to "feed the front end" is a chronic problem in the industry and one that strikes almost every new sales associate, and even top producers.

Think of a real estate transaction as a pipeline that starts with marketing yourself (the front end) and ends when you receive a commission check (the back end). For you to really sustain yourself in real estate, you need to keep as many transactions moving through that pipeline as possible, all at various stages of completion. And, unfortunately, you need to be working on every point of every transaction all the time that it's in your pipeline.

To use another analogy, you've seen the guy at the circus who spins the plates on top of the poles, constantly running from pole to pole trying to keep everything in motion. Well, in real estate, you're the plate-spinner. What often happens is that when new sales associates start getting a few nibbles, they find themselves pursuing those leads relentlessly, letting whatever other marketing they are doing slide. All they can see is the one or two deals that are almost within reach. They stop farming, stop calling their sphere-of-influence list, stop interacting with the people around them.

If they do manage to bring those deals together, they tend to redouble their focus to make sure nothing comes unglued before closing. They stop running from pole to pole and concentrate only on a couple of plates, leaving the rest to crash to the ground. What they are neglecting is the system that got them those deals in the first place. Real estate careers, like cars (the analogies just keep on coming!), do not work well if they are run briefly at 100 mph and then thrown into Park. Managers and trainers advise that you simply cannot forget to keep up with your call list even while nailing down your first couple of deals. You need to continue to do the basics.

This is not, of course, a problem that plagues only new sales associates. Many top producers find themselves having the best year of their lives, with multiple deals closing every weekend, only to come to work some Monday morning with nothing in the pipeline. No calls to make. No appointments to meet. Nothing to schedule. Truly successful agents always have the next deal somewhere in the pipeline and another deal right behind it. It all starts by making sure the front end, your personal marketing, is always working.

Drifting Away

Another key observation of many top managers is that when new sales associates start faltering, they start distancing themselves from the office. Agents who were showing up for work at 8 A.M. the first month start showing up at 9 and 9:30 the second month. Appointments with supervising brokers may be missed without a really good reason. Sales meetings will be skipped. They just can't make this week's broker tour.

Whether these agents know it or not, they are beginning to lose interest in their careers. In a profession that is largely self-regulated in terms of the hours put in and the days per week on the job, managers say it soon becomes apparent that the new sales associates are drifting away.

The Invisible Agent

Managers often identify the problem long before the sales agents do. Not unusually, drifting sales associates start by "rewarding" themselves for working so hard last week by not working so hard this week or by taking a day off to recover from some rejection. Instead of spending two hours making calls, they'll call for only an hour and spend the rest of the time reading about some "Brand-New, Can't-Miss" sales techniques.

What these things amount to, say trainers, are excuses to not interact with your career; to not interact with people you may be thinking are "better" than you, "smarter" than you, too "demanding" of you, or just plain "more successful" than you. Somewhere deep down, of course, you know these are just excuses.

For at least the first year, you need to dedicate yourself to making the office sales meetings, keeping your supervising broker up-to-date on what you're doing, and dragging yourself into the office every day. Especially for new associates, trainers say, real estate needs to be treated like a job.

It is important to occasionally take a step back, to try to view your life with greater perspective and remember what you are trying to accomplish here—and that's earn a decent living for yourself and your family. There is never a need to measure yourself against others. Your only need is to measure yourself against your own expectations.

The Never-Ending Client

Another bad habit new sales associates tend to fall into is working with the never-ending client; the client who for some reason has responded to one of your marketing pieces but never really intends to buy or sell a house. These are people who chew up time, but they also can form a curious relationship with an agent. In the back of your mind, you know this buyer is never going to find the right house or will never be ready to list. But the agent will find it more comfortable to continue working with the never-ending client than go out and pursue real business. In short, the sales associate convinces himself that if he's busy, he must be making money. The reality is that you may be busy, but you're not productive. Production is the only thing that counts.

The best way to overcome the phenomenon of the never-ending client, say sales trainers, is to work closely with your supervising broker or anyone else who can be ruthless in helping you go over your contact list. A good supervising broker will ask the hard questions: Is this person going to list or not? Is this person going to buy or not?—and he or she will require you to make an honest appraisal.

Very often, you will find yourself moving that never-ending client to the bottom of your contact list and moving better possibilities higher. Some clients lead to business, some clients lead to a comfortable rut. Real estate is a business, it's not a comfort zone.

Don't Take a Second Job

Most sales managers and real estate professionals agree that it takes a good deal of courage to go into real estate in the first place. Getting a license and dedicating your life to the business is the equivalent of believing that you are resourceful enough to make a living wage for yourself, by yourself, and that you don't have to be a gear in someone else's employment machine.

Taking a part-time job elsewhere, even to "get over the rough spots," is a substantial dent in that dedication and self-confidence. No matter how much you think it's only a temporary paycheck, it almost always is the first step out of the business. When you take a part-time job, nothing good happens. In fact, four very bad things are guaranteed to happen:

1. You are taking time away from the kind of self-promotion and marketing that may ultimately bring that steady stream of commission checks that all sales associates dream of.
2. If you're working part-time somewhere else, it means you're only working part-time in real estate. Full-time real estate professionals do not like to work with part-timers because it shows a lack of dedication to the business. And full-time professionals, of course, are the only ones you really want to work with because they typically are the only ones working high-quality transactions.
3. You'll lose business. Who would hire a part-time agent if they can get a full-time agent for the same price?
4. Maybe most important, if you take a second job, suddenly the wrong things become easy. Suddenly, at the end of every two weeks, there's a paycheck in your hand. Not much income, you'll say to yourself, but at least it's there without doubt. You have something definite to show for your work. If you have been a long time without income, soon you'll start asking yourself why you should risk your livelihood on real estate when you can make a full-time paycheck without the worry. Once you start down that road, it's hard to come back. Self-employment is not for everybody. Some people can't live without a safety net.

Something, however, drove you to get a license in the first place—and that something may have been the freedom to develop your full array of talents. Trust yourself.

A Few Self-Help Tricks

- The best way to get out of a real estate funk is not to get into one in the first place. Sales trainers say one of the best ways to keep yourself excited about the business is always—read that, always *always* **always**—have something you have to get done tomorrow. Write it in your day planner. Underline it. Have something to do with your business that you must get done the following day. If you have several things on your list, put the easiest thing at the top so you can make sure you accomplish it early and start your day on a positive note.
- Plan something to do with your business a couple of weeks from now:
  - Register for a sales class.
  - Plan to attend a local Board of REALTORS® event or a state meeting.
  - Contact the manager of an apartment building and see if you can hold a seminar for tenants on the benefits of home ownership.
- Set up an appointment with your supervising broker. Review what you're doing and ask your supervisor for suggestions. Urge your supervisor to stay in touch with you, to monitor your progress with you. In other words, if you have a hard time being accountable to yourself, demand that you be made accountable to someone else.
- Make yourself meet someone in the business whom you don't know. Try to get a few minutes of time with a top producer in your office to see if he or she needs some help with an open house or extra sign calls.

J o e   K l o c k ■

"The Deadly Dozen"

Joe Klock, the former head of Coldwell Banker University, is one of the great sales motivators in the nation. One of the things he urges both managers and sales associates to watch out for are what he calls "action stoppers," words or phrases that can kill your enthusiasm. As an interesting exercise, suggests Klock, put a check mark beside each of the following that you've said, or even thought, in the past few weeks:

__ It won't work.
__ I don't have time.
__ Let's think about it.
__ We've tried that before.
__ That'll cost a lot of money.
__ My customers are different.
__ I've got enough to do already.
__ I'm doing OK without getting into that.
__ It's never been done that way.
__ Let's form a committee.
__ If it's such a great idea, how come it isn't being done?
__ Maybe tomorrow.
__ I'm too (old)(sick)(tired)(late) to start it now.

Says Klock, "You need to drive the 'Deadly Dozen' out of your vocabulary, and steer clear of people who use them. Chances are, such folks aren't going anywhere you'd like to be. Chances are, they aren't going anywhere at all!"

(And yes, he knows there are actually 13.)

Reprinted with permission of Joe Klock, *www.joeklock.com.*

Chapter 21

You've Just Been Asked To Commit a Crime. What Do You Do Now?

Fair housing: The shortest distance
between you and the exit

This chapter is short because I'm in a race with your atten- tion span. When you say the words *fair housing* to new real estate agents, their eyes tend to glaze over. They think to them- selves, "I know all that stuff, I heard it all back in my prelicense class," and they don't want to hear it anymore.

So this reminder will just be quick and blunt: As a new agent (and even as an old agent), fair housing law problems also are your supervising broker's problem.

If you think a fair housing question has been suddenly dumped in your lap, do not try to handle it alone. You are risking your business, *and* you are risking your broker's business. And while your broker may not mind it if you risk *your* business, he or she probably does not want you to risk the entire company.

There's an old saying that's true even though it's old: "Million- dollar problems are rarely caused by million-dollar questions. They usually are caused by two-bit mistakes."

If you ever are on a listing presentation and a homeseller off- handedly says to you, "Just don't sell my house to a black family" (or Hispanics, or Jews, or single mothers), here's what you need to do:

1. Immediately break off the conversation, announce in clear and unmistakable terms that the seller is asking you to commit a crime, and that neither you nor your company engages in housing discrimination.
2. Leave.
3. Immediately contact your supervising broker, tell him or her what happened, and wait for instructions.

No matter how desperate you are for a listing or how tempted you are to take a chance you won't get caught, a fair housing law violation is a poison pill that can do a lot of damage to a lot of people. If you accept the listing and provide even a hint that you'll comply with the seller's wishes, you can (and probably will) be fired from your job, lose your license, and be sued down to your socks by every local housing discrimination group in town. And that doesn't begin to describe what the federal government can do to you.

Not only that, but your broker also can lose his or her license and almost certainly will be sued down to his socks by all those same people *and* the federal government—and he wasn't even at the listing presentation.

Look at it like this: Whether you accept or reject the listing is simply not your decision to make. It's not even your broker's decision. Congress already has decided discrimination is illegal, and it has dedicated millions upon millions of dollars to lawyers and housing groups to make sure you comply.

Your feelings about the law are irrelevant. The seller's feelings are irrelevant. *Fair Housing*, as they say, *is the Law*.

When "No" Is Not Enough

But saying "no" may not be saying enough. Be prepared to write down your recollection of the conversation with the seller, because even if you reject the listing and walk away, the issue still may not be over.

Depending on what your brokerage company's policy is, you and your broker may need to advise the government of what's happened. Why? Because the government thinks like this: By rejecting the listing yourself you have taken only the first step toward Fair Housing enforcement. Although you have decided not to be a party to the discrimination, the government may want to know what you did to prevent someone else, like the next listing agent who walked in the door, from participating in the discrimination.

In other words, even if you decide not to become involved, if your silence allows the discrimination to continue, you may still have some liability.

Twisting the scenario only somewhat, if you've just put your "For Sale" sign up in a seller's yard and a neighbor comes over to tell you not to let any minorities buy the house, your steps are equally clear.

1. End the conversation and advise the sellers what the neighbor said.
2. Advise your supervising broker of the conversation immediately and await further instructions.

Biased Buyers

Having said all that, it needs to be pointed out that the situation is less clear on the buyer side. When a buyer say, "Just don't show me any properties in a _____ neighborhood," he hasn't necessarily done anything wrong, other than reveal his personal prejudice. While it is against the law for a seller to discriminate against others, it is not against the law for a buyer to discriminate on his own behalf.

In years past, the exclusive buyer brokerage franchise The Buyer's Agent posed a similar scenario to lawyers at the U.S. Department of Housing and Urban Development, and the response was (how does one put this gracefully?) reluctant.

After distilling out a lot of the legalese, what it came down to was this: Real estate agents are not social engineers. It is not your job to make the buyer a better person by trying to insist that he live in a minority neighborhood.

HUD was very clear on several things, however: Real estate agents should *never* automatically assume that a buyer of any race, religion, national origin, and so forth, prefers one neighborhood over another. That's steering, and that's illegal.

Also, real estate agents should neither initiate a conversation about nor actively solicit the racial, religious, national origin, or similar preferences of the buyer, nor should they participate in conversations that suggest prejudice against one group or another. In other words, you may work to meet the stated preferences of your client but you may not lead him in those preferences.

A far more likely scenario on the buyer side goes like this:

You've just shown your African American clients another broker's listing. You're back outside and your clients are driving away in their car, while you remain behind to chat with the listing agent. Suddenly, a neighbor appears and advises you in no uncertain terms not to allow your clients to buy the house.

Now what do you do?

The unfortunate reality is that this scenario plays out more often than you'd think, and you could very well encounter it in your career.

> **Step 1:** Talk to your supervising broker and go over office policy.
> **Step 2:** Hopefully, that office policy will urge you to get in touch with your buyers immediately and simply and honestly explain what's happened.

In 90 percent of cases, your client is going to say, "Well, I don't want to live near some bigot. Let's look elsewhere." Should you urge your client to file a complaint with HUD? That's an option, but follow the lead of your supervising broker. Should you file a complaint even if your client doesn't want to? That's an option, too, but it's almost never a good idea to get ahead of your client on this kind of issue.

Again, you, your supervising broker, and your client all need to be on the same page on the issue.

A Real Estate Agent Is a Bus

A bus stops at the corner and opens its door. Anyone standing on the corner can get on as long as they have the correct change. A cab driver, on the other hand, can refuse to pick up the person waving wildly on the corner.

A rarely discussed fair housing issue is whether, and to what degree, you have the right to choose whom you want to work with. That is, are you a bus or a cab? It is best if you base that decision on money, rather than on race, religion, sex, or any of the other protected classes. If you want to list only homes costing $250,000 or more, that is your right. If you want to represent only clients looking at homes with prices of $200,000 or higher, that also is your right. To that extent, you're a cab. But once you represent a white client buying a $100,000 home, but then refuse to work with an African American buyer wanting to buy in the same price range, a discrimination question can be raised. Best advice: Set financial standards about whom you will work with, and stay with those standards.

Chapter 22

The Future: Lots of Questions, No Answers

Everybody sing! "Oh the times they are a-changing"

H ere's the downside. Everything is about to change. Yes, everything. Well, not how many square rods there are in an acre, but everything else. Gone. Kaput. Not going to be the same anymore.

But here's the upside: You could have made that same statement any time in the past ten years and been dead-on accurate. The real estate industry is in a state of transition right now, and don't let anyone fool you, nobody is quite sure where it's going to end up.

What property defects do you have to disclose to a buyer? What exactly is a property defect? What is your agency relationship with the buyer and seller? Are you even going to have an agency relationship? What about getting paid? Is that going to change? Is there a chance that your next continuing education class will be entitled, "How to be a banker"? There are some interesting times ahead.

Property Disclosure

Property disclosure issues have haunted the real estate industry for the past several years and it's going to get worse—or better, depending on which side of the transaction you're on. It will be important for you to keep up with the laws because property defects lie at the heart of the vast majority of lawsuits against real estate agents and their companies.

In the early '90s the rule was caveat emptor, "buyer beware." There were not many laws that forced a seller to disclose problems with a property. If buyers wanted to put an inspection contingency in the contract, they could. But that only meant the buyer was entitled to know whatever the inspector could find out. And inspectors, then and now, couldn't see through walls and couldn't look into pipes.

Now disclosures are everywhere. If you or your sellers know that radon seeps into the house, it has to be disclosed. If you know there is lead-based paint in the house, federal law says you must disclose that. And even if you don't know whether the house has lead-based paint but you do know that it was built before 1978, then you have to disclose the possibility that it could have lead-based paint.

Add to these the matter of sex offender disclosures. The law of the land now is that communities are entitled to know when a sex offender moves into a neighborhood. But what about families who buy into a neighborhood after the sex offender has lived there awhile? Is the new family entitled to know that a potential threat to their safety lives in the neighborhood? If they are, whose job is it to tell them about that threat? Is it going to be your job as an agent to keep up on where sex offenders live in the area you "farm" so that you can warn buyers? And if so, what rights do your sellers have? They're not the guilty party. Why should the value of their home drop just because a sex offender has moved in next door?

And that raises another question. In the past several years, required disclosures have moved from the "four corners" of the property to . . . who knows how far? In the early days of property disclosure, agents were only obligated to disclose things that were within the perimeter of the property: essentially, specific problems having to do with the house. In more recent times, however, agents have been called on to reveal far more than just what they know about the particular patch of dirt being sold and the house that sits on it. In California, mandatory property disclosures already go well beyond the four-corners rule. Homesellers must reveal earthquake fault lines, mudslide areas, and brushfire-prone areas.

There already has been a lawsuit that decided homebuyers were entitled to know that an abandoned landfill dump was located a half mile away. Residents feared the landfill would leach toxic chemicals into groundwater that could contaminate the neighborhood. The judge didn't say, however, how much agents needed to know about the surrounding areas, nor did the judge define how big a territory a "surrounding area" was. One mile? Two?

Likewise, noise pollution has become a terrible problem in some neighborhoods. Buyers who visit homes only on weekends won't necessarily understand how noisy a neighborhood can be during the week. Likewise, will agents have to disclose noise levels from nearby airports, depending on shifts in the flight path?

Disclosure of mold in homes almost certainly is on the near horizon for homeowners as more lawsuits stack up concerning the toxic growth. The presence of "synthetic stucco" coverings on homes, which has proven to contribute to the rotting of houses from within the walls, will have to be disclosed. There continues to be talk about electromagnetic fields (EMFs, commonly found around electric substations and high-tension wires) and whether they are a health hazard to homes near them.

Ultimately, what the legislatures, courts, and consumers are going to have to decide is whether consumers are entitled to surprise-free homes when they engage in real estate transactions. The reality is that the likelihood of ever having every possible disclosure met is far-fetched, at best.

The equally unrealistic alternative is an intense, prepurchase interview of the buyer during which every concern, phobia, and allergy is confessed. "How close would you mind living to a nuclear power plant?" "How many times do you sneeze during a day and why?" "Do you believe in ghosts?" "And now that we're done with this, will you refer your friends to me?"

Not likely.

Agency

Agency law, the law that defines your relationship with your clients and customers, also is undergoing dramatic upheaval. The common law of agency is becoming a little like an obsolete religion, still practiced in some places but superseded almost everywhere now by statutory agency. Most states have passed legislation defining the relationships between buyers and their agents and sellers and their agents.

The old law of "subagency" is almost gone and dual agency is on the run. Subagency, of course, was the old theory that the agent who worked "with" the buyer was actually working "for" the seller. At one time that was the common way real estate was practiced. Today, the word *subagency* has the same ring to it as "The world is flat."

Likewise, "dual agency" is on the run. Dual agency is the theory that one person can represent the best interests of both the buyer and the seller at the same time. While popular throughout the '80s and '90s, dual agency is now frowned on. Homebuyers, for instance, are wondering how an agent can promise to help them get the lowest possible price on a house while at the same time promising the sellers to get the highest possible price for them.

Dual agency is being replaced by "designated agency," in which, on an in-house sale, the supervising broker appoints one sales associate to represent the buyer and another one to represent the seller. The theory is that neither agent will reveal confidential information to the other. How well that will work remains to be seen.

For a new agent, however, designated agency is a problem. How can you, as a new agent, convince someone to list their house with you, saying "My supervisor will help guide the transaction all the way" if, in fact, the supervisor is forced into a mute position if a buyer comes in and starts working with another agent in the office?

And, of course, don't forget transactional agency, in which the agent represents no one in the deal but acts only as a facilitator.

One of these days you may be asked to take a course on how to do "nothing" for the customers, and do it right.

Some people even wonder if the day will come when consumers will develop agency relationships with Web sites. As sites get more elaborate and sophisticated in helping consumers find everything from a house to a school to a mortgage, at some point consumers are going to feel they have developed a relationship with a company, even though they have never met a human being at that company. Figure that one out.

Commissions

More and more, commissions are fair game. Discount brokerages are springing up everywhere promising to reduce commissions by full percentage points or more, saying new technology allows them to be more efficient and the savings are passed on to the consumer. Will full-service companies be forced to reduce their commissions to compete? Will so-called 100-percent-commission agents be willing to reduce their fees?

The role of the Internet and elaborate Web sites is, once again, relevant. Homebuyers who go online and are able to narrow the search down to just one or two homes by themselves, may be inclined to wonder what the buyer agent did to deserve to get paid.

Or will there be commissions at all? As discussed in other parts of this book, some companies are considering salaried agents, and there is some movement toward paying agents on a cafeteria basis: Showing a home will cost a buyer a specific amount. Putting an ad in the classified section of the newspaper will cost a seller a specific amount. Some people are quite comfortable already with that notion.

Banks in Brokerage

Finally, in the not-too-distant future, some people believe that almost all real estate companies are going to be owned by banks, rather than by brokerage companies. If the government does allow banks in, how will the industry change? Will agents be forced to live with banking regulations, and will they be better or worse off? For that matter, will you suddenly find yourself being trained in numerous disciplines to provide the consumer truly full service: Helping them find a house, a mortgage, title and homeowner insurance?

Mike Gorham ■

Looking into the Future

Fortunately, by the time that happens you will have taken control of the real estate industry. It's hard to tell what the future holds for real estate, but Mike Gorham, for 25 years the director of real estate in Colorado, believes there are six things on the horizon that the industry will have to deal with in the next five to ten years.

1. *You will be doing brokering all over the world.* "All the barriers to doing business around the world are falling, and they are crumbling pretty quickly. The large real estate companies and especially the banks want to be able to do business between states and between countries without a lot of licensing impediments. Pretty soon, if you get a license in one state, you'll be able to do business around the world without repeating common requirements."

2. *Transactions will be paperless.* "More federal and state laws are going to encourage paperless transactions. Today, people walk away from real estate transactions with two and a half inches of paperwork on each side. In the next decade, consumers will walk away from the close with a CD-ROM that has a complete record of the transaction—every piece of paper from the listing agreement to the closing documents will be on CD-ROM, complete with signatures."

3. *States and countries will develop uniform processes for transacting business.* "Once people are licensed to do business everywhere, and technology makes it possible to speed up

the deal, states are going to have to make the real estate process the same everywhere. States are going to have to come up with a common decision on agency, on whose contract to use, and the processes of closing the transaction. If we don't, the federal government will become involved in state regulation. It's already a concern in the insurance industry. It's going to happen in real estate, too."

4. *The managing broker is a business manager, not a day-to-day supervisor.* "More and more, the managing broker cannot micromanage the conduct of every agent who works for him. Agents are working out of their homes. They are making deals on cell phones and laptop computers. The supervising brokers aren't seeing the deals. They are losing more and more control every day, that's the reality of the business. As a result, there is going to be more education to make sure agents are responsible for their own conduct."

5. *There will be fewer of you and more unlicensed specialists.* "You look at what's going on in the business. The team concept of a licensed agent working with licensed or unlicensed assistants is coming on very strong. Today we have assistants drawing up the CMAs, someone else showing the property, someone else arranging the loan. There are going to be fewer actual licensees, but they are going to manage the transaction. The managing broker will be held responsible for new licensees and be responsible for the heart of the fiduciary responsibility: Entrusted funds, accounting, office policy, risk reduction and proper record-keeping."

6. *You are going to be dealing with a more diverse population.* "As we become more global, and more people from other parts of the world come here, agents are going to have to be more flexible about how they do business. They are going to deal with different languages, cultures, and ways of doing business. You are going to have to get used to it."

Chapter 23

First, Get Moose and Squirrel

The shortest distance between you and success

W hen I was a kid growing up, I used to watch the *Rocky & Bullwinkle* cartoon show. My favorite parts were always the story lines involving the evil Boris Badenov and his slinky companion, Natasha Fatale, the archenemies of the moose and squirrel. Boris and Natasha were every bit as sinister and cunning as Rocky and Bullwinkle were gentle and innocent. Every week, Boris would devise some devious, ingenious, and absolutely foolproof plan to take over the world. Every week, he would explain his marvelous plot to Natasha, but invariably he would end his scheming with these fateful words: "First, get moose and squirrel." Boris, of course, never got moose and squirrel. He never succeeded at world domination. Somehow, the bumbling Bullwinkle would always manage to foul things up and come out on top.

I used to think then how foolish Boris was.

Why didn't he just proceed with his plan and deal with moose and squirrel later? Why didn't he see that the shortest distance between him and success was a straight line, and the surest way to defeat was to start with a distraction?

As I've grown older, I have come to know Boris better. He is not so different from a lot of people, possibly including you, and certainly including me.

We form grand plans in our heads, and we are ardent in our desire to pursue those goals. But first, we just have to deal with this one "other thing."

That one thing could be anything. Maybe it's "just as soon as I pay off a few debts" or "as soon as I lose 20 pounds." Or maybe it's making sure that everyone else in the family is on their path to happiness before you launch yourself onto your path to happiness. All those things, in one way or another, are a decision to, "First, get Moose and Squirrel." They are self-made sidetracks and obstacles that keep us from doing the things we really want to do. A lifetime of living has convinced me of this: The time is never going to be right. The circumstances will never be perfect. The ducks will never be in a row.

You might as well start your new life today because if you don't, tomorrow won't be any different. But if you do set on an ambitious course today, I'll guarantee you that tomorrow will be different. If you've read this book at all closely, you see that you have a very tough several months ahead of you.

If you were to follow every guide laid out here, if you were to heed the advice of every top producer, you would be on the phone every morning, attending salesmanship classes during lunch, visiting neighborhoods for the rest of the afternoon, going to volunteer functions in the evening.

Home? Where's that? Spouse? Children? What's a weekend?

Nobody really expects you to pursue that course. Yet, a course approximates the track that may lead you to more success soon. The downside of that means that over the next year you can expect to have some arguments with your spouse, probably over time and money. You can expect to miss your children and a lot of their events. Just keep this in mind: Almost everyone quoted in this book already has been through what you are about to go through. They have been there and done that, and they have emerged on the other side of that year of darkness a much more skilled, confident, and competent individual. No matter how bleak the stories, the reality is that every voice heard in this book is doing quite well in the real estate business. They survived and you will, too.

Success in real estate, and most everything else, is the result of a three-part process:

1. Devise a plan.
2. Move forward.
3. Do it now.

Of those three, the "do it now" part is by far the most important.

A good plan without action will always fail. A bad plan with enough work often succeeds. If you want to be a success, *you* need to put *you* in motion. And once you're in motion, you are going to find some surprising things: Your family wants you to succeed, your broker wants you to succeed and, in fact, the entire real estate industry is prepared to open its doors to you. The first thing you have to do is step forward.

Forget Moose and Squirrel.

Do it now.

Here's a list of some common terms used in real estate. For more terms and more precise definitions, see: *The Language of Real Estate* by John W. Reilly (Dearborn)

Agency relationship An agency relation is the legal relationship you have with clients and customers. An agency relationship means sales associates are legally obligated to protect and assert the best interest of their clients. In nonagency relationships, sales associates may put another party's interest ahead of a customer's interest. For instance, a listing agent has an agency relationship, including fiduciary duties, with his or her client, the seller, but may still assist a buyer so long as the buyer's interest does not conflict with the seller's interest.

Agent An agent is someone who represents a consumer in a real estate deal. That consumer may be either the buyer or the seller. An agent is someone who will look after the interest of the consumer. **Note:** Despite popular use, the terms *agent, broker* and REALTOR® do not all mean the same thing. *See* broker; REALTOR®.

Arbitration A legally binding method of settling after-the-fact disputes between homesellers and homebuyers, between consumers and their real estate agents, and between the real estate agents themselves. Arbitrations between real estate agents typically involve which agents should be paid in a real estate transaction. Arbitration is less expensive than filing a lawsuit. The decision of the arbiter usually is final. *See* mediation.

Block busting A fair housing term used to describe the illegal practice of real estate agents trying to convince homeowners in a neighborhood that one or more members of a racial minority have moved into the community and warning that housing prices will decline as more minorities move in. Agents have used the tactic to convince homeowners to put their homes on the market right away.

Board of REALTORS A local Board of REALTORS® comprises all the REALTOR® members living within a geographic boundary, for example, the Seacoast Board of REALTORS®. The local membership elects officers. The various local boards then join together to form state REALTOR® associations, which then join the National Association of REALTORS®.

Broker A broker is someone who has received additional state-required training so that he or she may act as a supervisor over sales agents.

Broker, associate An associate broker is a sales agent who has taken the necessary additional training to become legally responsible for the purchase and sale of real estate but has elected to remain in the sales force, rather than become an administrator or manager over sales associates.

Broker, employing Someone who has taken the state-required training necessary to manage and supervise sales associates who participate in the purchase and sale of real estate.

Broker, owner A broker owner is someone who not only supervises the actions of sales associates but also is the owner of the real estate company. Not all company owners are "brokers" (but individual state laws differ). Many real estate company owners do not actually have real estate licenses themselves.

Broker, supervising A supervising broker is one who is actually liable for the acts of the sales agents who work in the office.

Broker's open An open house that is restricted to real estate agents. A broker's open allows agents to preview a home to determine whether it is right for clients.

Buyer's agent A buyer's agent is someone who is legally obligated to represent the best interests of his or her client, the buyer.

Calling, cold The practice of making unexpected calls to people you don't know in case they are interested in either buying or selling a home.

Calling, warm The practice of making unexpected calls to people with whom you are acquainted or contacting people you don't know but who have in some way, via the Web, 800 number, billboards, or other company marketing, expressed an interest in real estate services.

Caravan Many brokers from one or more companies touring homes that are available for sale. *See* broker's open.

Certification Generally speaking, a certification comes as a result of real estate training that helps someone function in a number of different real estate disciplines. For example, Certified Residential Specialist (CRS) certification involves training to help agents work with consumers who are both buying and selling residential real estate. It differs from a designation, which covers training in one specific discipline of real estate. *See* designation.

Certified Residential Broker The CRB is a special certification offered to real estate brokers that includes extensive training in the management of sales associates and operation of real estate offices and companies. The CRB organization is affiliated with the National Association of REALTORS®.

Certified Residential Specialist The CRS is a special certification offered to real estate sales associates after completion of extensive educational requirements involving the listing and marketing of homes. The CRS organization is affiliated with the National Association of REALTORS®.

Client A homebuyer or homeseller who usually has signed a contract agreeing to work with a specific real estate agent and has agreed to terms of compensation provided in the contract.

Code of Ethics A document prepared by members of an organization that states how those members should work with clients, customers, and each other as either colleagues or competitors. The National Association of REALTORS®, National Association of Exclusive Buyer Agents, American Society of Home Inspectors, and many other groups have codes of ethics.

Commission The percentage of a sales contract that goes to a real estate brokerage for selling a home. A 6 percent commission on $100,000 would be $6,000. Typical commission rates range from 4.5 percent to 7 percent. They are not set by law.

Commission, regulatory Every state has an agency, bureau, commission, or department that is legally responsible for licensing and regulating real estate license holders. The agencies include supervisory boards typically appointed by governors that include both members of the public and members of the industry. Those boards may review disciplinary actions and suggest new regulations.

Commission, split Most real estate agents receive payments based on the sales price of a home. A 6 percent commission on the sale of a $100,000 home equals $6,000. The money is then split again between the listing brokerage company and the real estate company whose agent brings the buyer. For instance, a 50/50 split between the companies would give each company $3,000. The agents who actually worked with the buyer and the seller each receive a portion of the $3,000 their companies received. If the agents split 50/50 with their companies, the agents would receive $1,500 each.

Commission payment *See* commission, split.

Comparative market analysis A comparative market analysis (CMA) is a document prepared by a sales associate to show homesellers what other homes—similar in size, neighborhood, or both—have sold for over a recent period of time. CMAs help sellers establish an asking price for their homes.

Continuing education Almost every state now requires real estate agents and brokers to take additional education after they have received their licenses. CE usually involves attending certain specified classes, earning a specific number of credit hours, over a specific number of years in order to keep their licenses active.

Customer A customer is someone a real estate sales associate works with, usually without a contract. Customers typically offer no assurance to agents that they will be paid for their work, forcing agents to seek their compensation elsewhere. For instance, if a buyer declines to sign a buyer agency contract, the sales associate may have to ensure his or her compensation through the listing agent.

Designation A designation is awarded after education is complete in a single discipline of real estate. For instance, skills learned in earning the Accredited Buyer Representive designation are focused on the benefits to homebuyers. *See* certification.

Desk fee A fee charged in so-called 100-percent-commission offices that defrays the expense of commonly used tools and services, including such things as photocopiers, telephones, fax machines, and so forth.

Disclosures Disclosures are items that, by law, must be revealed by buyers, sellers, real estate agents, lenders, and others. Sellers, for instance, must reveal certain problems, such as leaky roofs, to homebuyers. Agents must reveal their agency relationship to clients or customers before proceeding with negotiations. Lenders must disclose how much homebuyers are actually paying for homes they purchase.

Door hangers Sales associate marketing materials usually placed by hand on doors by going from door-to-door in neighborhoods.

Errors and Omissions insurance Insurance coverage for transactions that go wrong after-the-fact. May cover liability and legal costs. Real estate agents often are billed for all or part of their E&O insurance.

Exclusive buyer agent An exclusive buyer agent is someone who works only with homebuyers and does not list homes at any time.

Expireds Homes that may have had a listing contract on them for a period of time, such as 120 days, but have now had that contract expire. After the contract has expired, another agent may inquire about relisting the house with his or her company if the owner still wants to sell.

Facilitator A real estate license holder who does not legally represent the interests of either the buyer or seller but whose duty is to help the transaction come together by making sure forms are signed and filed where appropriate. Typically, facilitators do not negotiate on behalf of either party, nor do they recommend prices or offers.

Fair housing laws Federal and state laws that stipulate that homes must be sold to anyone who can afford them, regardless of race, color, religion, national origin, sex, familial status (including children under the age of 18 living with parents or legal custodians, pregnant women, and people in the process of securing custody of children under age 18), and disability.

The federal Fair Housing Act covers most housing. In some circumstances, the act exempts owner-occupied buildings with no more than four units, single-family housing sold or rented without the use of a broker, and housing operated by organizations and private clubs that limit occupancy to members.

Farm A "farm" is where you hope to grow your business. It may be a geographic area such as "the north side of town" or "all the homes in Shaker Heights." But your farm could be the Rotary Club, the country club, or all the families whose children attend the local elementary school. A farm is the place where you focus your marketing efforts first.

Fee-for-service The concept that an agent should be paid for services rendered, regardless of whether a deal closes. Agents may charge an hourly rate or make a la carte charges on such things as providing a CMA, showing specific properties, or holding an open house. Agency responsibility ends as the specific task ends.

Floor duty Known by various names, it is the work performed by an agent in the office who fields calls from consumers who are not already working with agents.

For Sale by Owner (FSBO) Properties whose owners are attempting to sell them without assistance from a real estate professional.

Graduate, REALTOR® Institute Basic training for real estate agents. Usually the first advanced training course received by sales associates who are members of the state REALTOR® association.

Gross commission income Total amount of commission dollars received by a company before splitting with sales associates. A preferred measurement in determining the size of a company. For example, "XYZ Realty earned $25 million in gross commission income (GCI), a 25 percent increase from the year before."

Homeowner Someone who has title to a property and is legally entitled to sell it.

HUD The U.S. Department of Housing and Urban Development, which is involved in many facets of real estate, from promoting and enforcement of fair housing laws to fostering an environment for the creation of lending programs for low-income Americans.

Independent contractor Most sales associates in real estate are considered independent contractors, meaning they are free to develop their business and work habits inside the framework of their company.

In-house listings The term *in-house listing* is used when referring to a property listed by one sales associate in a company that another sales associate in the same company may have a buyer for. There sometimes are bonuses given to agents who sell buyers in-house listings.

Inspector A home inspector is someone who checks a property for defects. Not all home inspectors are licensed, and in most states special training isn't even required to become a home inspector. Some, but not all, home inspectors are bonded. Asking whether an inspector is a member of the American Society of Home Inspectors (ASHI), which has standards of practice, is a good place to start in deciding whom to recommend.

Lawyer, real estate Not all lawyers are the same. It is best to recommend that clients and customers have "real estate attorneys" review contracts.

Leads A "lead" is simply the name of someone who may be interested in buying or selling a house. Leads come from the contacts you make inside your sphere of influence. The company you're working for may have its own "lead generation" system in which people call in response to advertising. Those leads may be available for you to follow up on.

Lender A lender is a bank or a company (or even an individual) that actually risks its money by making a loan. *See also* mortgage broker.

Listing A listing is a house for sale by a real estate agent. When the owner of the home agrees to allow an agent to sell it, the owner will sign a "listing agreement," a contract that outlines what the agent will do to market the home in exchange for how much of a fee.

Listing agent A listing agent is the agent who has a signed agreement with the person selling the house. *See* selling agent.

Manager Someone who usually, but not always, holds a real estate license and is in charge of office administration. A manager may also be an owner and supervising broker.

Mediation A nonbinding method of settling after-the-fact disputes between homesellers and homebuyers, between consumers and their real estate agents, and between the real estate agents themselves. Mediations can involve anything from what fixtures are to be conveyed in a deal to the discovery of undisclosed defects. Mediation tends to be an informal way to resolve disputes. However, parties are not barred from going to court if the mediation is unsuccessful. *See* arbitration.

Mentor Someone in an office who will explain policies and procedures as well as demonstrate some sales skills to a new agent. Mentors also may be authors and seminar speakers who provide guidance to brokers and sales associates.

Model home A model home is one of the first homes a builder will construct in a new housing development. The home is used to show buyers basic floor plans and typical features of homes that will be built in the development.

Mortgage broker A mortgage broker is someone who helps homebuyers sort though loan packages offered by various lenders. *See aslo* lender.

Muliple-listing service The Multiple-listing service (MLS) is a collection of most, if not all, of the homes listed for sale by MLS members within a certain geographic area. The listings are collected in a central database that can be searched by other members of the MLS who have buyers interested in purchasing a home of a specific style or in a specific location. Membership in a REALTOR® organization is no longer required to participate in an MLS.

National Association of REALTORS® The National Association of REALTORS® (NAR) is a trade association of some 800,000 members. The NAR owns the word *REALTOR®* and prohibits its use by real estate licensees who are not members of the trade association. The NAR has a very active political lobby in Washington and in state legislatures around the country to help lawmakers define business dealings between real estate license holders and other industries. Its political lobby also attempts to protect property owner rights by defending such things as the mortgage interest tax deduction.

Niche A niche usually defines the specific expertise of a sales associate. A niche could be first-time homebuyers, luxury homebuyers or vacation homebuyers. It could be a specific section of town. Or it could be properties within a specific price range, for example, "Laura's niche was the $250,000 to $600,000 market."

Open house A home for sale held open for public visitation by either the listing agent or an assistant for a specific number of hours.

Owner Someone who owns a real estate company. May or may not have a real estate license.

Procuring cause The real estate professional responsible for a sale. On the buyer side, the agent who procured the sale may be the agent who introduced the buyer to the property or the agent who actually got the buyer to make a purchase offer. Disputes over procuring cause by members of the National Assocation of REALTORS® are usually settled through arbitration.

Production The total amount of property sales made by an agent or by a company, for example, "Sally sold a $200,000 home and a $350,000 home for production this month of $550,000."

Prospecting The act of searching for customers.

Protected class *See* fair housing law.

Rainmaker A slang expression for a person in the office who brings in clients and then usually hands them off to other associates.

Real Estate Buyer's Agent Council The Real Estate Buyer's Agent Council (REBAC) is a subsidiary of the National Association of REALTORS® and trains members in how to work specifically with buyer clients. Its primary designation is the Accredited Buyer Representative (ABR).

Real Estate Settlement and Procedures Act The Real Estate Settlement and Procedures Act (RESPA) is a federal law designed to protect consumers in real estate deals. RESPA establishes under what conditions referral fees may be paid when brokerages send business to lenders and title companies and what kind of disclosures must be made to the consumer if the lender and title company have either common ownership with the brokerage or some other affiliation.

REALTOR® A REALTOR® is a member of the National Association of REALTORS®, a trade association that acts on behalf of the nation's real estate sales force. Membership is voluntary, but most real estate companies do belong to the group. Only people who are members of the organization may call themselves REALTORS®.

Referral fee Money either paid or received in the transfer of business from one brokerage to another. "Mary received a referral fee from Jim (in a distant city) for sending him a client who wanted to buy property there."

Salaried agents Sales associates who are paid a salary and receive benefits. The majority of sales associates are paid on the basis of a percentage of the contract. *See* commission, split.

Sales associate A real estate license holder. The entry-level position for most real estate agents.

Selling agent The agent who brings the buyer to the deal typically is called the *selling agent*. Under certain circumstances, the selling agent may also be the *buyer's agent*.

Sides This refers to which side of the deal you are on. If you are helping the seller you are on the "seller side," and if you are helping the buyer you are on the "buyer side." One of the ways to measure your success is "how many sides" you do per year— the total number of sides represented in the course of a year.

Sphere of influence The sphere of influence is the group of people real estate agents normally depend on for business. Such a sphere may include family and friends, neighbors, and members of social clubs or civic organizations.

Subagency An agency theory that stipulates that the sales associate working with the buyer is actually a subagent of the listing agent, and therefore information gathered by the subagent about the buyer may be legally passed on to the listing agent. Subagency, in vogue in the '80s and '90s, has been abandoned in most states.

Supervising broker A supervising broker is the person who keeps agents in line. This is the person agents turn to for help in terms of sales, legal issues, and even just plain office administrative questions.

Title insurance Required by most lenders before a mortgage can be approved. Title insurance guarantees that the property is free of claims from unknown third parties, such as former spouses or workers.

Top producer A real estate agent who is among those who make the most money in a real estate office.

Tour day *See* broker's open.

Transactional broker Like a facilitator, a transactional broker is said to "represent" the transaction only. Transactional brokers safeguard the legal transfer of property from buyer to seller but without giving negotiating advice to either side. *See aslo* facilitator.

Volume *See* production.

Women's Council A council affiliated with the National Association of REALTORS®. Open to both men and women, the WC provides leadership training for real estate agents and brokers.